Hire Right, Higher Profits

The Executive's Guide to Building a World-Class Sales Force

By Mr. Lee B. Salz

ISBN: 1493762621
ISBN 13: 9781493762620

DEDICATION

To my amazing children, Jamie, Steven, and David…

You will learn many things along life's journey. One thing that no one can teach you is passion. That's a quest you must pursue on your own. It is my hope that each of you finds the passion that leads to your eternal happiness.

ACKNOWLEDGMENTS

It is often said that it takes a village to raise a child. The same can be said for the development of a book. *Hire Right, Higher Profits* would not be possible without the support of my team.

Subject Matter Expert Advisors

- Dawn Deeter-Schmelz, J.J. Vanier Distinguished Professor and Director, National Strategic Selling Institute, Kansas State University
- Donna Kirtz, sales management practitioner
- Mike Moroz, former president of Archway Marketing
- Rick Olson, CEO of KRM Information Services, Inc.
- Susan Savage, Majority Owner and CEO, Sacramento River Cats – Triple-A Baseball Team of the Oakland A's

Editors

- Sharon Salz
- Myra Salz
- Henry DeVries
- Sandra Livingston

My sincere thanks and appreciation to all of you for your time and assistance with this book.

To both my wife, Sharon, and my mother, Myra, thank you for challenging me throughout this process and making *Hire Right, Higher Profits* everything I dreamed it could be.

A special thank you to my support system. They stand behind me during all of my life's personal and professional ventures.

- My wife, Sharon Salz
- My parents, Joseph and Myra Salz
- My sister, Marlo Salz
- My in-laws, Paul and Gail Pershes

TABLE OF CONTENTS

ABOUT THE AUTHOR

Mr. Lee B. Salz is a leading sales management strategist and expert in hiring and onboarding highly profitable salesforces. Through his sales management consulting firm, Sales Architects, Lee has helped hundreds of companies experience explosive growth through the migration of their sales teams from "people-based" to "process-based." An expert in hiring, onboarding, management, coaching and compensation, he designs the programs companies need to cultivate and maintain high-performance salesforces.

In addition to *Hire Right, Higher Profits*, he is the author of three best-selling business books: *Soar Despite Your Dodo Sales Manager* (WBusiness Books, 2007), which won the silver medal in the Top Book Awards; *Stop Speaking for Free! The Ultimate Guide to Making Money with Webinars* (Business Expert Publishing, 2010); and *The Business Expert Guide to Small Business Success* (Business Expert Publishing, 2010). He serves on the Editorial Advisory Board of *Sales & Marketing Management* magazine, is the host of the *Sales Management Minute* podcast series, and is the chairperson of the *Sales Management Challenge* executive skill-development program.

Lee was recognized as one of the Top 25 Sales Influencers by OpenView Labs in 2011 and 2012, and is a member of the Top 25 Online Influencers in Talent Management (HR Examiner 2011). His articles have been published in hundreds of websites and magazines. He's been interviewed on ABC News and MSNBC, and has been quoted and featured in many leading publications, including *CNN, The Wall Street Journal, The New York Times, The Dallas Morning News,*

Selling Power magazine, *and Sales and Marketing Management* magazine.

To help companies implement the sales enablement methodology presented in *Hire Right, Higher Profits*, Lee launched *The Revenue Accelerator*® – a web-based, sales onboarding and enablement technology firm. The firm's technology platform has been used to onboard thousands of salespeople – resulting in shorter ramp-up times, higher revenue production, and reduced sales turnover.

Lee is a results-driven consultant, dynamic speaker, and passionate entrepreneur. He lives in Minneapolis with his wife, three children, and two dogs. When he isn't helping companies grow, Lee can be found on the baseball field coaching his kids or in the gym preparing for his next powerlifting tournament.

You can learn more about Lee Salz on his websites:

www.SalesArchitects.com

www.TheRevenueAccelerator.com

For speaking and consulting engagements, contact Lee at lsalz@salesarchitects.com or 763.416.4321.

FOREWORD

To those of us who study sales performance for a living, ineffective sales hiring is indisputably an epidemic. You know there's a real problem when researchers agree that the attrition rate among B2B salespeople hovers around 25 percent, while nearly 50 percent of salespeople don't deliver on their revenue targets. We also know that, depending on the industry, somewhere between a fifth and a third of salespeople aren't suited to the roles that they were hired to perform. That means that no matter how much technology, coaching, training, support, incentives, and assistance you provide, they will never make their numbers.

It doesn't take an advanced degree in mathematics to see the cost of this. Billions of dollars are squandered every year by companies paying people who can't get their jobs done, resulting in a never-ending succession of lost business opportunities.

Sales managers who don't realize that hiring is a skill – a series of actions and behaviors driven from a formal process – are destined for failure. The facts speak for themselves: the tenure of a vice president of sales in the U.S. averages only 19 months. Surround yourself with salespeople who can't get their jobs done, and you won't be able to do yours. There is no way around that equation.

Contributing to the problem is the spate of bad advice about hiring salespeople from self-proclaimed experts who need no more than a computer and internet access to promote their (quite likely unsubstantiated) points of view. I feel badly for the sales managers who understand the hiring challenge and seek out a solution in earnest, only to find that they have put their own jobs, or even their careers, at risk.

In *Hire Right, Higher Profits*, Lee Salz deftly demonstrates that the hiring epidemic results from a widespread lack of knowledge, misdirected business perspective, and a tactical, short-cut mentality on the part of sales managers, VPs, and senior executives. Then he presents us with a hiring solution. And it's not just a theory; it's a proven strategy that has not only worked in the past, but also works right now, and will continue to work for anyone with the discipline to take the right steps, even if it's for the very first time.

Ineffective (or, more commonly, non-existent) onboarding is another scourge preventing the building of high-performing sales teams. Even if you were to hire a salesperson with the right skills, connecting his or her skills to role proficiency through a mutual investment by the salesperson and the company in the form of a formal onboarding program is a must. Lee makes a strong financial case and gives you all the knowledge and tools you need to integrate onboarding, done the right way, into your operation.

If you can accomplish what Lee lays out here – hiring salespeople who will excel in their roles, and onboarding them effectively – you will have overcome one of the biggest business challenges facing sales managers and executives today. You'll be in the rare position of building a sales organization where 80 percent of your team delivers 125 percent of the revenue target – a far cry from today's lackluster standards for performance.

As if all of that weren't enough, Lee frames his hiring and onboarding approach as the investments that they are, giving you what you need to run that component of your sales operation like the business that it is.

A bit of advice…Check your ego at the door, forget what you think you know about hiring, and open your mind. Then turn the page and learn from a master.

Dave Stein
Founder & CEO
ES Research Group, Inc.

1

THE TEST MOST EXECUTIVES FAIL

Albert Johnson comes home from work exhausted. He hugs his wife and kids, and then he falls into his easy chair. Today was just another grinding day for him as the vice president of sales for The Magic Mirror Company. The tremendous pressure to achieve the corporate revenue budget number sits on his narrow shoulders. Things are tough right now and he is being squeezed by the CEO as well as his executive peers to drive sales.

As he leans back in his chair, Albert scratches his head in search of a way to get the revenue boost the company needs. After spending a few hours deep in thought and watching *King of Queens* reruns, he dozes off without ever touching his dinner. His thoughtful wife covers him with a blanket, takes the kids to bed, and leaves him to sleep in his chair for the night.

The next morning, Albert wakes up with a start. He has just come up with an incredible idea to drive sales. He reaches over to the coffee table for a pen and pad and begins to scribe his thoughts. "This idea is going to revolutionize our business," he thinks. "Revenue will sky-rocket, profits will soar, and I will be a hero."

Albert can barely contain himself as he springs out of his chair, show-ers, dresses, and heads to the office. *Screech!* His tires skid as his car comes to a quick stop in the corporate parking garage. He leaps out of the car and sprints to the CEO's office without even stopping to drop off his laptop and coat.

As he reaches the CEO's office, he briefly pauses to catch his breath. Wiping the sweat from his brow, he enters and declares, "I've come up with a great idea for us to drive revenue and take our business to the next level. We will take the competition by storm."

Albert shares the idea with Linda Austins, CEO of The Magic Mirror Company. After listening intently, she leans back in her chair and says, "Interesting concept ... How much will it cost to implement this revenue-growing idea of yours?"

"It's only a $25,000 investment!" Albert says.

In an instant, Linda goes from sitting back in her chair to leaning across the desk toward Albert.

"Did you say $25,000? That's a lot of money! You've seen our financials and I'm sure you're acutely aware of the current economic climate."

Albert interrupts, "I know it's a major investment, but I am also confident it will drive profitable revenue for us."

Linda rises from her chair, walks over to the window, and stares for what feels to Albert like an eternity. Then she looks back at Albert and says: "Albert, I'm intrigued. Here's what I need you to do. Write up the idea and send it to me in an email. Research the concept and see what the marketplace thinks of it. After you have done that, put together a blue-ribbon panel to conduct a feasibility study. Of course, talk with Finance and Operations to get their take on this idea as well. Once you have gathered all of this information, put together a presentation for the team. We should be ready to make a decision on this idea within six months to a year. Now, keep in mind that a $25,000 expenditure is not taken lightly around here, Albert. Great job coming up with this idea."

With those marching orders delivered, Linda turns to her PC and begins reading her email. Albert finishes writing down his to-do list and packs up his briefcase. As he begins walking toward the door, he stops and turns to Linda.

"I almost forgot to mention this to you," he says. "I'm going to extend an offer to a sales candidate today and invite her to join our inside sales team. I interviewed her yesterday and she looks like a good fit. Do you want to meet her?"

Without even looking away from her computer, Linda replies, "Nah, that's okay. What salary are you going to offer her?"

"$25,000," Albert responds.

Still without looking away from her email, Linda quickly says, "That's fine."

While this story is fictional, I envision a knowing smirk on your face because this scenario rings true in your company. The Magic Mirror Company analyzes (perhaps, even overanalyzes) a $25,000 investment in an idea intended to increase revenue, but pays little mind to hiring a salesperson with a $25,000 salary whose job is to increase revenue as well.

Here's the point many executives miss... *It's the same $25,000 investment!*

Even that statement isn't completely accurate. Hiring a salesperson at a salary of $25,000 doesn't cost the business $25,000. There are additional costs that compound this expenditure such as health insurance, other employee benefits, and travel. To be truly accurate, a percentage of the sales manager's cost to the company should be allocated to the salesperson expenditure as well. And, the $25,000 in this scenario is an annual salary, not a one-time cost to the business. Even though many salespeople are paid annual salaries significantly higher than $25,000, executives rarely view the investment in an idea the same way as the hiring of salespeople.

If your firm operates like The Magic Mirror Company, it just failed the *Revenue Investment Test* – by viewing an addition to the sales team as merely hiring, and not as an investment in revenue. Companies taking this approach risk incurring huge and unnecessary costs in the forms of high turnover, underperformance, and lost sales.

But top-performing companies view their sales teams in a completely different way. They recognize that each salesperson represents a revenue investment made by the company. To make informed, investment decisions, each candidate goes through a structured, deliberative evaluation process. While the adding of headcount is commonly called "hiring," these companies view it through the lens of investing in revenue. While *revenue investment* is a common business expression, the usage of it in this book refers to each member of the sales team. When executives adopt the revenue investment perspective, the entire way they view their current and future sales teams change.

For example, they don't just analyze the sales pipeline; they also scrutinize the *sales candidate* pipeline. These executives know that only searching for talent when they are staring at open seats on their sales teams can result in poor selection decisions. Instead, they are perpetually on the lookout for talent and always have prospective candidates in the pipeline.

In addition, these executives, before evaluating candidates, analyze the sales role to develop investment criteria. Those criteria are used to develop a multi-step candidate evaluation process. Those candidates, in whom a revenue investment is made, participate in development programs to help them get up to speed rapidly leading to a fast, high return on the investment.

These executives also understand that salespeople contribute to both sides of the company's profit and loss statement. It's absolutely true that the sales force is a source of revenue. But it also represents significant costs, both tangible and intangible, to the business. While you can easily tabulate the tangible ones, it is much more difficult to quantify the intangible ones – like the brand damage resulting from sales turnover and sending the "salesperson of the day" into accounts.

The philosophical shift from *hiring salespeople* to investing in revenue is a key to driving both top-line and bottom-line sales performance. This book provides the practical guidance needed to implement this strategy in your company and cultivate a highly successful and profitable sales force. The corresponding methodology and processes presented have been implemented in companies of all sizes and in most industries. They work for all because they can be adapted to specific business environments, needs, and cultures – as you are about to see.

2

THE MYTH OF THE GREAT SALESPERSON

Years ago, my wife Sharon and I adopted a dog from a local shelter. We knew nothing about his background other than that he was estimated to be about three years old. "Hello Newman!" Newman is the name your dog is given when the husband, who is a huge *Seinfeld* fan, gets naming rights for the family dog. He came into our home that first day and somehow knew all of the rules of the house. He never had an accident, never damaged anything, and slept while we ate dinner. Newman was the perfect dog.

Several years later, Sharon thought Newman needed a companion and suggested getting another dog. Since training a dog is easy (given the Newman experience), I was completely onboard with the idea. So, we adopted Baby. Baby is the name given to the dog when your daughter gets the naming rights.

Baby's background was also a mystery, but that was the end of the similarity between our two dogs. Her first few weeks with us were a total disaster. She charged the door every time the doorbell rang. She dug up our backyard and ripped the gutter off our house while chasing a chipmunk. And for some odd reason, she picked a random spot on the wall in my daughter's room and clawed a baseball-sized hole in it.

A series of these incidents got the best of me. I grew frustrated and angry. Sharon became upset and disappointed. This was not at all what we expected given the experience with Newman. We were close to admitting that we had made a mistake and even considered returning Baby to the shelter.

As a last-ditch effort, Sharon suggested trying a dog training service to see if that would change Baby's behavior. *Eureka!* After four weeks of working with the trainer, Baby was miraculously transformed. She now had better skills than Newman. Baby had become a completely different dog. *(By the way, Sharon gets all of the credit for this.)*

Why include this story in a business book on profitably growing a sales team? This dog story parallels a belief that has been instilled in the minds of executives. They believe that somewhere there is a *great salesperson* fully formed and ready to be discovered. Executives wander the earth in search of these creatures and often come away feeling duped. The problem is, just when the executive thinks he has found a *great salesperson* (the kind who will produce millions of dollars in revenue while the executive masters his golf swing), the salesperson fails.

Every once in a while, lightning strikes and a company finds a *great salesperson*, just like we found Newman. But this is the exception, not the rule. More commonly, companies find salespeople who are more like Baby – they arrive with potential, but both of you have work to do for that potential to become reality.

Some of you may have read that last section and still buy into the *great salesperson* belief. If you are one of these people, I pose this question to you:

> How many of these so-called *great salespeople* have you hired – people who came equipped with a great track record, polished appearance, terrific prospecting skills, and fantastic closing skills – but they failed in your company?

If you still believe in *great salespeople*, then you must also subscribe to one of the following given their failure:

1. These salespeople completely forgot how to sell when they arrived at your company.

2. Your company is the absolute worst company to sell for in the history of business.

What other reason could there be other than these two given the belief in *great salespeople*? Sales management life would be just perfect if prospecting and closing skill proficiencies were the sole measures of salesperson greatness. And, if they were the sole measures, how would you explain a rainmaker in one company failing miserably in another company? Or, a sales dud from one firm becoming a sales star elsewhere? You couldn't.

The issue is the placement of the word "great." *Greatness* is not a standalone quality, but rather a synergistic attribute of the relationship between the salesperson and a specific sales role in the company.

In top-performing companies, the objective is not simply to hire salespeople or search for *great salespeople*. These companies do something far more beneficial and impactful. They hire right; they put a laser focus on finding the right salespeople with the potential to be great in specific sales roles for the company. You know my mantra (I like it so much that I made it the title of this book): *Hire Right, Higher Profits*.

Anecdotally speaking, here's what I've found during my years of building salesforces:

Five percent of all salespeople will SUCCEED under any circumstances.

There's a word for this type of salespeople – entrepreneurs. These people aren't walking the streets looking for sales jobs. They are building businesses. They are rarely part of the talent pool.

Five percent of all salespeople will FAIL no matter what is done for them.

These are individuals who need to be counseled out of the sales profession. They don't have the makeup for a career in sales.

Ninety percent of all salespeople fall into the LIMBO group.

Their success or failure is determined by two factors.

1. The strength of the match between them and their sales roles.

2. The sophistication of the company's new-hire development program – to help them quickly and effectively use their skills and know-how in a new environment.

This is not a scientific study so don't look for a quoted source. However, during more than twenty-five years in the sales management trenches, I've seen a deceptively simple formula work time after time.

Identify candidates with the potential to succeed in specific sales roles
+ Offer skill-development programs to turn potential into reality
Higher Profits!

So where are the right candidates found? They can't be found if you don't know what is needed for success. The first step is to fully scope the role. In essence, the expression "right salesperson with the potential to be great" for a specific role in the company needs to be defined. This is done by identifying the factors that cause people in that role to succeed or fail.

You may have noticed that I've included the expression "specific role" a few times when referring to the scope rather than just saying "potential to be great in your company." The reason is each sales role, even within the same company, is unique. The factors leading to a candidate's success or causing underperformance/failure are different for every sales role.

Many executives believe that their competitors are an excellent source for salespeople with the potential to be great. If your company is among the many whose recruitment strategy boils down to hiring from the competition, read on. The next chapter may very well change your mind.

3

HIRING FROM THE COMPETITION: FAST GROWTH STRATEGY OR FLAWED SALES MYTH

Several years ago, I ran a sales organization in the technology-training industry. This was during the Dot-Com Boom Era when Microsoft, Novell, and Cisco were taking information-technology back offices by storm. The never-ending technological changes were dizzying, and the training industry was going gangbusters. We were minting money.

One afternoon, I received a call from a salesperson who worked for one of our competitors. He was calling for himself and five of his colleagues. They were concerned about the financial health of their company and wanted to join our team because we were doing so well. My first thought was that this call was a set-up, but it turned out to be the real deal. I had heard rumors about this company having issues, but cast them aside given the current state of the industry. I could feel myself beginning to salivate with the thought of hiring six salespeople from a competitor that had been a thorn in my side.

We scheduled interviews with all of the candidates and I sprinted to my general manager's office to share this incredible news. Like me, he was elated by this opportunity. We were ready to draft offer letters before ever meeting these salespeople. The GM and I began reforecasting our revenue projections and the conversation quickly turned to facility expansion. We were downright giddy.

The next day, we "interviewed" the six of them and all were hired on the spot. I say that we interviewed them, but neither my GM nor I heard a word they were saying. We just wanted these instant rainmakers on our team as we envisioned their impact on our growth.

We had them on the phones their very first day talking to prospects. After all, these salespeople came from the industry and had the expertise to sell technology training programs. At least, that's what we thought.

Fast forwarding ahead three months, all six of them had failed and were let go. Truth be told, it was our fault not theirs. We never should have hired a single one of them. We didn't pause, even for a moment, to consider if these salespeople had the abilities to succeed in our company. Had we not let sales giddiness get the best of us, we would never have hired any of them. We had been blinded by dollar signs that were nothing but a mirage.

We referred to their former employer as a competitor. Yet, in retrospect, while that firm was in the same industry, our companies were very different. Some of the differences were:

- Our company primarily sold to consumers while the competitor focused on corporate sales.
- We invited prospects to our office for a consultation while they sold accounts by phone.
- Our salespeople sold comprehensive programs while they sold individual courses.
- We were the high-price training company in the market. They played *Let's Make A Deal!* and always sold cheap.

Born with Industry Mastery

Looking back, it's so obvious that I should have carefully matched each candidate to the needs of the role. If I had, I wouldn't have been so quick to extend offers. That's the benefit of hindsight. I also know I'm not alone in making this mistake.

Executives often tell me that they always focus their salesperson recruiting efforts within their own industry. There is an executive perception (or better stated, a misperception) that industry knowledge cannot be taught. If that's true, it begs the question, "Did you come out of the womb knowing your industry?" Of course you didn't. You learned it just like the new salespeople can.

I've also learned the hard way that knowledge of the industry doesn't necessarily translate into sales success. Years ago, I took over the leadership of a sales team in the employment screening industry. Early in my tenure, I went on sales calls with each of our reps to see how effective they were in promoting our company's value proposition.

One of the reps I inherited had sold for several of our competitors in the past. When I traveled with her on a sales call, everything she said in the prospect meeting was factually correct. No doubt she knew the industry inside and out as well as the product fundamentals. However, there was a major problem. While everything she said was correct about our company, the same pitch could also have been made by any of the other industry players. She had no passion for our unique solution and it all sounded too vanilla. A salesperson's passion is a key motivator that drives prospects to buy. When prospects perceive vanilla, the only remaining differentiator is price. We were not the low-price provider so you can probably imagine how this story ends.

What's clear is that top-performing companies never presume that their competition has developed salespeople that can be poached, handed the phone book, and instantly sent on a revenue quest. Instead, they make a revenue investment in salespeople who fit the role, recognizing that skills can be taught.

These companies attract and cultivate top sales talent by tackling the "industry experience" concerns head on. As part of their overall recruitment strategies, they provide comprehensive skill and knowledge development programs guiding salespeople, without prior industry background, to succeed in their new roles. They don't limit themselves to candidates from within their industries.

The Book of Business – Dream or Reality

Executives make three key mistakes when they pursue candidates with industry experience. We've discussed two of them – the assumption that these candidates will have a fast ramp up and the misperception that success is guaranteed. The third mistake becomes apparent when the starry-eyed interviewer looks at the candidate and asks: "How much business can you bring with you?"

This is an awful expectation to set for a prospective salesperson. Very early in the courting phase, an ethical dilemma has been created for the candidate. If the candidate thinks it is unethical to take clients from his current employer, a negative message has been received and the relationship tarnished in the first few moments.

This question is directly tied to the executive dream of hiring a *great salesperson* who arrives with a huge book of business. But this dream seldom comes true. I realize some of you reading this may disagree with my perspective, so allow me to share my reasons.

First of all, let's be honest with ourselves. It's not easy to move a mass number of clients from one supplier to another. When a salesperson has left your company to work for a competitor, how successful was she at taking clients with her? She probably wasn't very successful.

I'd be skeptical of any sales candidates who claim to have that kind of power over their clientele.

There is a bigger issue at stake. Asking a candidate the "book of business" question also opens up an ethical Pandora's Box, not to mention potential legal issues. Her employer has paid some form of compensation for these clients and it is the employer – not the salesperson – who owns them. Thus, this question is a borderline request to steal from that company. Would you really want a person with that kind of character representing your brand?

Given that salespeople often change employers, this person will one day leave your company too. How do you think she will exit? As the saying goes, the best predictor of future behavior is past behavior. Do you really want that headache? Finally, if a revenue investment decision is made solely based on the "book of business" factor, what happens when the client pipeline runs dry?

Still not convinced of these potential perils? If you believe industry experience belongs in the candidate-requirements criteria, be prepared for another major issue to hit your business: *Scalability.* After all, there are only so many salespeople in your industry and only a small subset of them would be right for your company. What happens when you run out of sales candidates because the talent pipeline runs dry?

The Toughest Candidates to Evaluate

Candidates who have industry experience are often *fun* interviewees. Much of the interview time is spent hobnobbing about the industry, sharing war stories, and comparing lists of the people you both know. It's truly a delightful conversation.

Most executives tell me that they would not describe themselves as professional interviewers. This makes evaluating candidates with industry background tricky for them. An interview is the ultimate sales call, and sitting in front of you is a pro. Not only is this person a pro, he drops industry terms into the conversation and makes the exact points you want to hear.

These interviews are about as tough as it gets … for the interviewer. Few recognize when they are potentially getting duped. Actually, most think these are the easiest interviews because the traditional Q & A becomes a conversation with these candidates. While the conversation is enjoyable, you may as well wear a honey suit in a beehive because you are about to get stung.

After reading this chapter, you may think I'm completely opposed to making a revenue investment in someone with industry background. Not at all. I'm not advocating complete avoidance of these salespeople. However, I do encourage executives to remove the rose-colored glasses that cause them to hire salespeople who don't have what it takes to succeed in the roles. I can't emphasize it enough: Bad hiring decisions are, in reality, poor revenue investment decisions.

In the next chapter, you will learn how to fully scope a sales role by identifying the factors that lead to success, failure, or underperformance. Once that process is completed, you will be prepared to make informed, revenue investment decisions – whether the salesperson has prior industry background or not.

4

IDENTIFYING THE FACTORS THAT AFFECT REVENUE INVESTMENT PERFORMANCE

I regularly speak to CEO organizations about sales hiring and introduce the *revenue investment* concept as a strategy to grow sales teams rather than simply hiring salespeople. When beginning my talks, I ask the groups, "How many of you have identified and written down the attributes of your ideal client?" Hands are raised in earnest response to the question.

My follow up to that question is: "How many of you have identified and documented the attributes of your ideal salesperson?" Eyes dart away from me and the looks on participants' faces remind me of the elementary school students who don't want the teacher calling on them.

Companies spend thousands, if not tens of thousands of dollars, trying to determine the right prospects for their products. They hire firms to analyze their approaches, identify the buying audiences, and create strategies to reach those prospects. Yet, few employ the same level of scrutiny when seeking the right people to sell to those prospects.

The Executive Disconnect

When asking those same CEOs to share the attributes of their ideal client, I feel like a game show host as answers are shouted out. I can't write fast enough to capture them all. Changing gears, I ask them to share the attributes of the right salespeople for their companies. The hoots and hollers turn into a deafening silence.

After a few moments, which probably feels like an eternity to them, I break the silence and share what is commonly listed as the criteria of the ideal salesperson for a company:

- Excellent prospector
- Strong closer
- Very strategic
- Solution seller
- Value seller

The CEOs feel as if they're off the hook, but I'm just getting warmed up. "If everyone in the room agrees that these are the attributes of their ideal salesperson, then wouldn't every salesperson who meets these criteria succeed in their respective companies? It would stand to reason that this would be the case, wouldn't it?" That's when the CEOs start to understand.

There are factors – beyond selling skills – impacting performance in every sales role. A great example is the Dot-Com Boom Era hiring practices. Most Dot-Com companies failed and for a variety of well-documented reasons. However, there's one reason rarely discussed, namely the selection decisions they made when hiring salespeople. Those decisions also contributed to their demise.

Founders of these Dot-Com companies pursued salespeople from big IT houses such as Microsoft, Cisco, and Novell to sell for their small businesses. These executives were captivated by the prospect of recruiting rock stars from big technology companies. However, they painfully discovered that these salespeople often did not have the expertise to open doors and introduce new companies and products. Those salespeople had been successful selling in environments where they represented the *Big Kahunas*. However, when it came to introducing a new company or product for a lesser-known company, the salespeople were not equipped to do what needed to be done to succeed.

I had a great vantage point to see this in action as several of my friends left sales positions with huge, established firms to pursue roles with small, no-name startups that dangled stock options. As one friend shared with me: "When you work for Microsoft, you are a finalist in every deal – even if you have never met anyone in the company. Chief Information Officers rearrange their schedules to meet with you. Now, here I am working for ABCTechnology.com and calling on those same CIOs. Rather than receiving a warm welcome, I'm greeted with, 'Never heard of your company,' and I struggle to set a meeting." The huge stock option opportunities were beyond their grasp.

By now readers of this book may feel a bit frustrated. I've said that there is no such thing as a *great salesperson*. And, I've recommended thinking twice before pursuing the competitor's salespeople for your company. Given all of that, you are probably wondering who does belong on your sales team.

There isn't a one-size fits all answer to that question. Every sales role in every company is unique. No two are exactly alike. Before you can adeptly evaluate candidates, the factors that impact success need to be identified. Those factors are found through a *Revenue Investment 360* analysis.

The Revenue Investment 360

The *Revenue Investment 360* is the comprehensive process used to identify the factors leading to success or failure in the role. These factors are called "performance factors." The *Revenue Investment 360* goes beyond sales skills and scrutinizes every facet that impacts success. The reference to 360 is the connection to a 360-degree analysis which studies performance from every angle.

This process is conducted for each sales role in the company, as the performance factors vary for each one. For example, there are unique performance factors that impact roles such as inside sales representative, business development specialist, and account manager. Thus, each one needs to be fully scoped during the *Revenue Investment 360* process to best understand the factors unique to it.

The *Revenue Investment 360* role evaluation process is broken into three sections. The first is a role overview. The second examines the selling landscape. The third delves into the specific sales role's responsibilities for each of the various phases of the sales process. The responses to the questions in these sections provide you with the role's performance factors.

Part I: Role Overview

1. What attracts salespeople to want to sell for the company?
2. What keeps salespeople with the company long term?
3. How would you describe the sales culture of the company?
4. To whom will this person report and what is his management style?
5. What title will be offered to those in this sales role?
6. What administrative and sales support functions are offered?
7. Where is the office located for this role? (home, corporate, or field)?
8. What percentage of the time will this salesperson be away on overnight travel?
9. Other than sales, what metrics is this role held accountable for achieving?
10. How many sales is the salesperson expected to deliver in his first year? Second year?

11. What is the compensation plan for this position, including salary, commission, bonuses, etc.?

12. What will a salesperson earn, given the level of sales performance identified above, in his first year? Second year?

13. What benefits/perks are offered?

14. What are you willing to teach to a new salesperson?

15. What are you not willing to teach to a new salesperson?

16. What programs are in place to help the new salesperson get up to speed?

Part II: Selling Landscape

1. What solution is this salesperson responsible for selling? (i.e., tangible product, service, technology, or Software as a Service {SaaS})

2. Who is the ideal client for each of the solutions sold by this salesperson?

3. Is this role responsible for selling directly to the end user or building/managing a distribution network?

4. Is this salesperson selling to new prospects or up-selling/cross-selling to existing clients the company already acquired?

5. Is the solution marketed broadly or to a narrow niche?

6. Is the solution purchased one time or repetitively with this salesperson role involved/not involved?

7. Is the solution purchased in a standard, configured, or custom format?

8. Is the solution sold primarily by phone or in-person?

9. Is the sale usually completed in one sales call or over multiple calls?

10. What territory is assigned to this salesperson?

11. Is the sales territory well-cultivated or an expansion into an untapped area?

12. How well recognized is the company among the target buyers?

13. How well recognized are the solutions among the target buyers?

14. How well recognized is the company relative to these solutions among target buyers?

15. Is this role expected to create demand for this solution or does it already exist in the marketplace?

16. At what department/level is the ideal point of entry into a prospect organization?

17. What are the ideal circumstances to pursue a prospect for these solutions? (i.e., incoming lead, news story, etc.)

18. What departments/levels influence the buying decision?

19. What departments/levels usually make the final buying decision?

20. Is the primary decision maker also the ongoing contact person for the account?

21. On average, how long is the sales cycle from first contact to contract award?

22. What is the average sale size?

23. How would you describe the competitive landscape?

24. How is the solution priced relative to the competition?

*Note. The use of "solution" in the aforementioned questions is a generic way of referring to a product, service, technology or SaaS.

Part III: Role Responsibilities

Sales Process Phase	Describe the role's responsibilities for each of the following phases	How well-defined are the processes for each phase? (Well-defined, moderately-defined or undefined)
1. Account strategy		
2. Lead generation		
3. Needs analysis		
4. Concern/objection handling		
5. Solution development		
6. Proposal development		
7. Group presentations		
8. Pricing		
9. Account implementation		
10. Account management		

Oftentimes, the temptation is to have one person complete the *Revenue Investment 360* process. However, this exercise is most effective when it is collaborative. While you may be the sales leader, your peers may also have insights to share that affects revenue investment performance. You may even want to have a select group of senior members of the sales team provide input during the *Revenue Investment 360* process as well.

While the *Revenue Investment 360* has placed a wealth of information at your fingertips, the role-scoping analysis is not complete. Some feel overwhelmed by all of the data in front of them. The next chapter helps to resolve those concerns. It details how to use the information gathered in the *Revenue Investment 360* process to assemble a *Performance Factor Portfolio* for the role.

5

DEVELOPING THE PERFORMANCE FACTOR PORTFOLIO: THE INVESTMENT FOUNDATION

If you tried to find candidates who matched every performance factor identified during the *Revenue Investment 360* process, you would search forever without finding any. What is needed next is a review and prioritization of the performance factors based on their level of impact on success. The set of key factors become the *Performance Factor Portfolio* – the role's criteria list.

To contrast with dating, I'm sure at some point in your life you put together criteria for your perfect companion. Maybe you kept a mental list, or put pen to paper. As you recall the list, how many requirements were there? Five? Ten? Twenty? As you experienced the dating world and gave the list a reality check, the number of requirements was reduced – recognizing that some of the items on the list weren't requirements at all. They were "nice to haves." A companion with red hair may have been one of the original requirements, but would you really not have pursued a relationship with a blonde matching every other requirement on the list? For most, the red hair became a non-issue and was a "nice to have" rather than a "must have." In other words, red hair was a desired attribute, not a required one.

Coming back to the *Performance Factor Portfolio,* just like there are no *great salespeople*, there are no perfect ones either. If there were, the sales management profession would not exist. As the performance factors identified during the *Revenue Investment 360* are reviewed, the knee-jerk reaction may be to search for candidates who match every part of that scope. That's not going to happen for the reasons mentioned earlier. That means the next step is to determine the factors which most impact performance.

Required Versus Desired Attributes

Suppose there are twenty performance factors on the list from the *Revenue Investment 360*. The next task is to rank them in terms of the level of impact on a salesperson's success. The first one on the list is the most critical performance factor and the last one is the least critical. In essence, the criteria are prioritized based on the level of performance impact. This prioritization is not much different from what people subconsciously do when setting criteria for the companion they seek.

With the twenty factors ranked by performance impact, mark each one as either *required* (must have) or *desired* (nice to have). If this exercise is performed correctly, the lion's share becomes *desired,* while a select few at the top become *required*. It is the few factors that are deemed critical to one's success in the role that belong on the *required* list.

An introspective question that helps resolve the *required* versus *desired* issue is:

> If a candidate matches most of the *Portfolio*, but not a particular performance factor, would you still extend a job offer?

If the answer is "yes," a "nice to have" factor has been identified. If the response is "no," that factor is a "must have."

For example, "lead generation expertise" may be on the list of performance factors. In companies that are very active in product marketing, lead generation mastery may be a "nice to have" as they have the ability to make the phone ring for the salespeople. In companies that don't have the same level of product marketing, this performance factor is a "must have" because salespeople who cannot generate leads fail in the roles.

Another example of a performance factor for consideration is "office location." Working out of a home office is not the same as working out of a corporate office. Therefore, if someone has worked out of a corporate office for the last twenty years, the shock of working remotely may be untenable. The converse is also true. Someone who has been working remotely may have difficulty working in a corporate or regional office environment. The key is finding candidates who will thrive in this role's office arrangement.

By identifying the *required* and *desired* attributes, the *Performance Factor Portfolio* – the foundation when evaluating candidates – has been developed. Is this exercise tedious and challenging? It certainly is, but it's also invaluable. All of the sales training in the world cannot fix poor hiring practices.

Revenue Investment Scope Evolution

The *Performance Factor Portfolio* is not a static set of criteria, but rather evolves over time. For example, I was one of the first people in the United States to own a Blackberry. The first day they were available on the market, the Blackberry salesperson delivered mine to my office. I'll never forget that first conversation with him as he touted the virtues of "email on the go." The concept of having access to emails whether on the road or in meetings – away from my computer – was brilliant, which is why I bought a Blackberry. The salesman was masterful at introducing a new product and concept.

Imagine that same salesperson calling on me fifteen years later with that same approach of positioning "email on the go." I would have thought he was nuts. Why? The smartphone has become an integral part of the business professional's toolkit. Today, the "email on the go" concept is a given. The question we now face is how to select the right phone to suit our needs from among the myriad of choices. This is an example of a marketplace change that needs to be monitored in the *Performance Factor Portfolio* because the skills associated with introducing a new product are different from the ones needed when selling in a tough, competitive environment.

The Power and Peril of Sales Titles

When it comes to assigning titles to sales roles, executives often pay little mind to the inference associated with them. Yet, when a salesperson is handed her title, she immediately derives a message from it – and so will her clients. There are plenty of sales title options to consider so take time to pick the right one for the role.

One commonly used title is *account executive*. This title implies that the company has a well-defined strategy and process in place. It also suggests the position is a rank-and-file role filled by salespeople who are provided both an objective and a roadmap to achieve it. The one-word descriptor for the account executive is *executor*. Account executives execute the company's sales plan.

Another often used sales title is *business developer*. This title implies that the role is very creative. Business developers rarely get a roadmap from the company. Instead, they get an objective, and are expected to chart the course to achieve it. When I hear this title, I think Indiana Jones. "Here's the treasure we want. Figure out how to get it." The one-word descriptor for this sales role is *pioneer*. The business developer both creates the plan and executes it.

Executives may be tempted to offer the salesperson titles such as: *manager*, *director* or *vice president*. These titles send a "management message" to both the salesperson and her clients. And, it is highly likely that both parties misinterpret the salesperson's authority because of the assigned title.

To share a story, my family and I went out for dinner at a local restaurant, and it was an ugly experience. Fed up with all of the issues throughout the meal, we summoned the manager. He listened to the problems and sprang into action. After ensuring everything had been resolved, he handed us a bill with many of the charges removed without a request from me to do so. Needless to say, we will certainly return to that restaurant.

Why did I ask to speak to the manager? I believed, and correctly so, that he had the ability to quickly address my problems. Imagine if he came to the table, heard the issues, and said he couldn't do anything about it. How frustrated would we have been given his managerial title? And, we probably would have never gone back to that restaurant.

Companies commonly offer salespeople inflated titles such as *director or vice president* as a recruitment strategy or to promote someone in lieu of a higher salary. While I understand why executives use this approach, it can create a disconnect between titles and responsibilities leading to problems both inside and outside the organization. For example, an inflated title can lead salespeople to incorrectly believe they have the power to set pricing or make service-level decisions, when in fact their decision-making authority is far more limited.

Title also communicates authority and responsibility to clients. When service issues, contract language, and pricing concerns arise, people look to this "executive" as their savior. They become frustrated when they find out that he is merely a sales representative in disguise and unable to resolve the issues on his own. (Think back to the restaurant experience.) Before deciding what title to assign to this role, consider the message received by both the one given it and the people who hear it.

This chapter helped you precisely determine the *Revenue Investment Candidate* scope by prioritizing the critical performance factors and selecting the appropriate title for the role. That foundation provides you with the information needed to develop the campaign that attracts the talent you want. In the next chapter, you learn strategies to appeal to those candidates.

6

ATTRACTING REVENUE INVESTMENT CANDIDATES

Once *Revenue Investment Candidate* criteria are set, the next important step is drawing talent to the company. A marketing campaign is needed to attract candidates to the sales opportunity you have to offer. Many executives are not accustomed to thinking of recruitment in terms of marketing, but that is what is being done. Marketing campaigns for products are designed to attract a defined prospect type. That same mindset is needed to find the right investment candidates. This marketing campaign is intended to attract the specific type of prospects you want applying for the role.

Coming back to the *required* versus *desired* decisions made for the *Performance Factor Portfolio*, those choices affect the way the role is marketed. This is another reason to be prudent when determining the "must haves" list as those choices shape the scope of the marketing campaign. A massive list of *required* attributes in a job advertisement severely limits the number of candidates applying and makes outbound candidate searches (recruiters, job board searches, etc.) more challenging.

Job Board Snafus

A little hobby of mine is reviewing job boards to see how executives are attempting to attract top salespeople to their organizations. I often read ads showing a long list of attributes that candidates "must have" meaning that those are *required* to be considered for the role. However, when I reach out to executives and ask about the advertised positions, it turns out that many of the listed attributes really fall into the *desired* category. Not surprisingly, these are the same executives who say they are frustrated with their recruitment campaigns.

Employers publish job advertisements for the sole purpose of luring candidates to apply, but they undermine their own efforts by using the tool improperly. Instead of attracting candidates to apply, employers are convincing salespeople that they don't have the right stuff by inaccurately characterizing *desired* attributes as *required* ones. Below is an example of an elaborate list of *required* attributes from an actual job board advertisement.

The successful candidate must have:

- BA/BS with a focus on business or life sciences
- An MBA from a well-respected institution
- 10 years sales management experience
- 10+ years business-to-business sales experience with the Fortune 1000
- Broad knowledge of principles and methods in a recognized professional field, or working knowledge of multiple fields
- Well-versed in using CRM tools
- Experience selling based on a formal sales methodology is essential
- Must be good at developing and articulating ROI to C-level executives
- Telecommunications experience is a must

How many people match this entire list? Does anyone match all of these criteria? Would this company really not consider a revenue investment in someone who does not possess some of these attributes? By publishing an ad that is so restrictive, the company misses out on potential superstars who choose not to apply.

I've also had conversations with salespeople about their perceptions of a job advertisement and the listed requirements. One frustrated salesperson said: "I read the list of requirements in the job posting and if I don't have 100 percent of the posted background, I don't submit my resume because I won't be considered. So, why should I waste my time applying?"

On the other side of the fence, when I ask executives about the biggest corporate challenges they face, just about all of them cite "finding top sales talent" in their top three. Their challenge with finding salespeople could have its roots in what they've listed as requirements in their marketing tools.

Taking it a step further, don't wait for candidates to come to you. In other words, don't place a job ad and wait for candidates to apply to it. It's the same as hoping that product advertising will make the phones ring. Control your destiny and pursue potential revenue investment candidates. Don't wait for them to apply.

Both job boards and LinkedIn have tools to search for candidates by keywords. The *Performance Factor Portfolio* provides the words to use. Review the candidates' online persona and pursue candidates that match the *required* list. Send an email that tells a candidate that you reviewed his background and have an opportunity which may be of interest. Ask him to reply back to the email to begin the conversation. Just like salespeople shouldn't wait by the phone for prospects to call, sales managers need to have an outbound campaign to find revenue investment candidates.

Recruiter Frustration

This "must haves" issue isn't limited to candidates and employers. Recruiters are frustrated too. Clients provide them with so many restrictions that they feel handcuffed in their ability to find the right *Revenue Investment Candidates*. One recruiter said: "I really want to help my client, but I feel like I'm searching for a needle in a haystack. I don't dare send any candidates to them unless I find an exact match to what they've given me," he said adding, "I don't think they intend to be so restrictive, but that's what they have given me to work with."

Companies also undermine their recruitment efforts with catchall phrases that turn off candidates. I get a good chuckle every time I read a job board advertisement that includes "other duties as assigned" in the scope. In the history of business, no one has ever applied for a position because he saw he would receive the *benefit* of "other duties as assigned" if he were to join the company.

"Other duties as assigned" is important to include in a *job description*, where the company details the laundry list of possible responsibilities. However, the phrase doesn't belong in a *job advertisement,* which is a tool intended to attract top sales talent and get them excited about joining a company.

Who in the company is best equipped to create this ad? That work typically goes to the department that manages recruiting and hiring – Human Resources. Oftentimes, HR does not possess the expertise needed to develop creative advertising for job openings. There is, however, a department that specializes in attracting prospects – Marketing! Ask colleagues in that group to help craft the message as prospect attraction is their expertise.

When to Search

Executives often wonder when to recruit top sales talent. The best practices answer to that question is clear:

> There is one time, and only one time, that is best to search for *Revenue Investment Candidates*, and that is when you are not in need of any.

Only searching for them when slots are open on the sales team creates a high probability of moving too hastily and making poor investment decisions.

Nutritionists tell their clients never go to the supermarket hungry. They know famished people make desperate, appetite-driven choices. The same concept applies to revenue investment decisions. Sales leaders should not limit their evaluation of candidates to the times when they have open slots on their sales teams. It is the parallel to shopping while starving.

Desperate hiring is the result of sales leaders knowing that their annual revenue goal was based on the expected sales department headcount. If there are open seats, the math doesn't work. Each member of the sales team may meet his annual goal, but if the team is short on headcount, the department's revenue number is at risk. The fear associated with open cubicles and jeopardized revenue targets could lead executives to forget about the revenue investment concept and bring on someone – with a pulse and a smile – just to fill a chair.

When a salesperson is not achieving his revenue goals, one of the primary reasons is a dry sales pipeline. We all know that when a salesperson gets busy, the first task that gets jettisoned is prospecting. A sales team without a healthy sales pipeline is in big trouble when it comes to achieving revenue goals. The same risk holds true if another pipeline – the *Revenue Investment Candidate* pipeline – runs dry.

Just as salespeople are expected to prospect 365 days per year, sales management executives also need to be prospecting for candidates year-round. This helps to ensure that unemotional investment decisions are made. Not having a strong candidate pipeline has a major impact on both the top-line and bottom-line of the company. Sales leaders need to hold themselves accountable for maintaining this pipeline just as they hold their salespeople accountable for developing a strong prospect pipeline.

What happens if a candidate is found, and there isn't an opening on the sales team? The question is posed as a problem, but it isn't an issue at all. Sales management best practices tell us to always upgrade the bottom twenty percent of the team, which means there is always room for new, top talent. There's no excuse for not perpetually recruiting.

With the role defined and the marketing tools created, the next step is to put together a program to evaluate candidates against the *Performance Factor Portfolio*. That program provides the data needed to make educated, revenue investment choices for your sales team.

7

CONSTRUCTING THE REVENUE INVESTMENT EVALUATION PROGRAM

With the performance factors identified in Chapter 5 and potential candidates found through the marketing campaign shared in Chapter 6, how do you compare and contrast candidates with the *Portfolio*? That's where the *Revenue Investment Evaluation Program (RIEP)* comes into play. This program provides the data needed to make revenue investment decisions. The *RIEP* helps identify salespeople with the potential to be great in a specific role by highlighting the synergies (or lack thereof) between the candidates and the *Performance Factor Portfolio.*

There are a multitude of components to consider for inclusion in the *RIEP*. While several may be intriguing, select only those that are most helpful when identifying matches between *Revenue Investment Candidates* and the *Performance Factor Portfolio.* It's best to assemble a team to both develop the *RIEP* and help assess the candidates. By using a team approach, you get valuable input, buy-in, and consistency when evaluating candidates – all of which are vital to making investment decisions.

The balance of this chapter presents a series of *RIEP* components – from interviews to simulations – as well as how to best incorporate them in your company. Importantly, don't lose sight of the core purpose of the *RIEP,* which is to identify synergies between candidates and the performance factors. Only include those *RIEP* components that help with revenue investment decision-making.

Phone Interview

There's nothing revolutionary about a phone interview. Human Resources team members have traditionally been tasked with making calls to pre-screen candidates. But the phone interview conducted as part of the *RIEP* serves a different purpose; it tests candidates' phone skills.

In most sales roles, part of the prospect/client relationship is handled by phone. In some sales positions, the entire sales process is conducted by phone. In others, there is a mix of calls and face-to-face meetings. Regardless of how much of the sales process is telephonic, candidate phone skills should still be evaluated. Why? Looking at the *Performance Factor Portfolio*, I'll bet there are several factors related to phone skill mastery.

Obviously, phone skills can't be evaluated during an in-person interview. Thus, a phone interview is needed as part of the *RIEP* to evaluate the candidate's expertise. During this interview, structure the call so that the candidate's phone persona can be assessed. Is he comfortable on the phone? Is he upbeat or just plain blah? Can this candidate build a relationship on the phone? There will be some *Revenue Investment Candidates* you look forward to meeting in-person because they are so engaging on the phone. Imagine a prospect feeling that same way about a salesperson.

The converse is also true. If the salesperson exhibits a lackluster personality during a phone interview, how will that person perform when selling for your company? And how does that phone persona impact performance in the role? If this is a highly impactful performance factor, carefully consider whether or not to continue with this candidate.

When prospecting, salespeople reach voicemail much more often than they reach a live person. Given that, consider intentionally missing the candidate's call so he has to leave a voicemail message. Then, call him back immediately so that the appointment is not missed.

After the phone interview, go back and listen to the voicemail message and evaluate it for both content and tone. You may be raising an eyebrow questioning the necessity of this step. Considering the revenue investment associated with adding a salesperson to the team, wouldn't you want to analyze every aspect that affects performance?

What is assessed during the phone interview is a function of what was included in the *Performance Factor Portfolio*. In addition, some of the other elements to evaluate include:

- **Punctuality** – Did the candidate call at the agreed-upon time? Unless a major catastrophe occurred, lateness cannot be excused. It exposes his potential behavior with prospects and clients.

- **Diction** – Was the candidate well-spoken and easily understood? This person will potentially represent your company and your brand. If he cannot speak well, it can create a negative impression of the company.

- **Language** – Slang and profanity don't belong in the conversation. I cannot believe I have to mention this, but these days, candidates are becoming very familiar in the interview process. Having grown up in New York City and New Jersey, I'm not unaccustomed to brash language, but I am sometimes astonished by the inappropriate language some candidates use. This demonstrates poor judgment and raises concerns about how the salesperson will interact with prospects and clients.

  In one particular instance, I was asked to conduct a phone interview for a client. The candidate began the conversation by saying, "What's up, big guy?" I had never had any prior interaction with this candidate – and this is how he elected to begin the discussion? You can probably imagine my recommendation for "big guy" to the client.

- **Next Steps** – Top salespeople are accustomed to asking about the decision process and next steps when selling. The same expectation applies here. Did the candidate inquire about the hiring process and the decision-making criteria? If not, this could be cause for concern with his selling acumen.

- **Feeling** – How did you feel after the conversation with the candidate? Is this someone you are excited to meet? If not, this is probably not the right *Revenue Investment Candidate* to represent the company.

In-Person Interview

Just about every *RIEP* has an in-person interview component. While such interviews are common, they are not always handled effectively.

Do you know when most executives prepare to interview candidates? They do it as they walk down the hall to the conference room for the interviews. While this practice is commonplace, it is certainly not recommended. It is not uncommon for sales candidates to be better prepared for the interview than the interviewer.

When it comes to interviewing candidates, executives are always looking for the best questions to ask, but there is no perfect list that applies to all sales roles and companies. Given that, take the time to craft a consistent set of interview questions based on the *Performance Factor Portfolio*. Asking that set of questions provides the ability to compare and contrast responses. To get started on that list, I've included my *Top 100 Sales Interview Questions* in the Appendix of this book. Don't ask them all. Ask only those relevant to the role and that will help you identify synergies between the performance factors and the candidates.

In addition to the set of questions established to ask of each candidate, another set of questions is compiled from a review of the candidate's resume. (In Chapter 8, tips for conducting a resume review are provided.) Take the *Performance Factor Portfolio* and compare it to the candidate's resume. Look for matches and potential matches – as well as mismatches. Use the interview to identify matches, confirm potential matches, and talk through mismatches. Obviously, those questions can't be effectively developed while walking down the hall to the interview. Take the time to analyze the resume and prepare for the interview long before stepping into the conference room.

> Remember that the best sales interview questions are the ones that help determine if there is a match between the role and the candidate.

Similar to the phone interview, other elements to assess during an inperson interview include:

- Punctuality
- Diction
- Style
- Next steps
- Feeling
- Dress
- Note-taking – Taking notes is an indicator of a candidate's sincere interest in the role and potentially shows how he would handle a sales call.
- Questions asked – Genuinely interested and strong candidates arrive with a list of questions to ask.

Group Interview

The group interview may seem like a great addition to a *RIEP*, but it is very difficult to administer without proper planning. The group interview belongs in the *RIEP* if, as part of the sales process, salespeople work with prospect groups. This is an effective way to see how well the candidates handle the group personality and style dynamic.

For this exercise to produce the desired results, select a chairperson and determine who is asking which questions and who is responding to which questions. Define an end to the exercise, so that it doesn't go on for an eternity.

A word of caution, group interviews can easily turn into inquisitions and become a turnoff to candidates. Script this component carefully when electing to include it in the *RIEP*. Keep your eye on the core purpose of this process, and focus on questions that expose matches and mismatches to the *Performance Factor Portfolio*.

In addition to matches to the *Performance Factor Portfolio*, other areas to evaluate in a group interview include:

- Punctuality
- Diction
- Style
- Next steps
- Feeling
- Dress
- Note-taking
- Group Management – Did the candidate engage each of the group participants?

Simulation

A simulation also sounds like a great addition to a *RIEP*, but it can be difficult to execute. In a simulation, a candidate is placed in a selling situation such as a sales call or group presentation to evaluate performance. With a simulation exercise, the challenge is to determine what the candidate's performance indicates relative to making a revenue investment decision. If it doesn't tell something meaningful, then all it accomplishes is to stress out the individual, and there is no reason to include it in the *RIEP*.

There are two scenarios when it is prudent to include a simulation in the *RIEP*. The first scenario is for candidates who work for competitors or have other industry experience. Simulations provide the chance to see them in action. This may provide a better indication of their strengths and weaknesses than an interview, which as Chapter 3 explained, is akin to the ultimate sales call in which the pro is in his element.

Before the simulation, provide information to the candidate so he can prepare for the exercise. This is the knowledge that a salesperson would normally have prior to a needs analysis meeting. Since the candidate has industry background, this exercise is an evaluation of his needs analysis questioning and solution development expertise.

The other time when it is helpful to include a simulation in the *RIEP* is in a business-to-business sales environment that requires salespeople to create solutions based on a prospect's requirements. Once the candidate has been through the core of the *RIEP*, so that all pertinent information relative to the role has been shared, ask the candidate to put together a five-minute presentation. That presentation should explain why he is the right person for this investment. Through this approach the candidate is exposed to your revenue investment philosophy, which then helps him understand how he would be held accountable if asked to join the team.

Since an interview is a form of a sales call, hopefully, the candidate has asked questions to learn what the company is looking for in the right person for the role (needs analysis). He certainly knows himself (the product). The presentation is the communication of the solution – the synergy between the role requirements and his expertise. This simulation gives the ability to see the candidate's creativity, presentation prowess, and speaking skills. Be strict about the five-minute allotment so you can evaluate his sales effectiveness when given a tight timeline.

Included in the Appendix are sample score sheets to help you successfully incorporate simulations in the *RIEP*.

Assessment

It is worrisome when I hear companies are using assessments as part of their *RIEP*. If you use assessments today (or sell them), that statement has probably caught your attention. Before rushing to judgment, let me explain. My concern is not the science behind these assessments, but rather their use in the revenue investment decision-making process.

Most assessment tools are intended to provide sales talent evaluators with candidate data. They are not recommended to be used as the ultimate hire/no-hire decision. Yet, many executives do not use these tools in the way their designers intended.

What often happens is that everything looks great with the candidate, but the assessment tool gives an unfavorable report and the company ends the *RIEP*. If you are going to be that reliant on the assessment, there's no need for any other part of the *RIEP*. Why bother investing time in interviews if you are going to take such an extreme approach with the assessment tool? If the candidate passes, make an offer. If he fails, eliminate him from the process.

Assessment tools can be used productively if they provide additional data points to contrast candidates with the *Performance Factor Portfolio*. These tools certainly help confirm matches and expose mismatches. The mismatches indicate that there's more conversation to be had with the candidate. The identified concerns may end the consideration for a *Revenue Investment Candidate* or they may become irrelevant after further analysis.

Reverse Interview

The reverse interview is a great way to help candidates understand the role for which they have applied. It is called a reverse interview because the interviewer doesn't ask any questions. This is the time for the candidates to ask any and all questions of someone who has been successful in the role for which they are being considered.

During these interviews, the questions asked by the candidate are the measurements. Given that the candidate has been offered a wonderful opportunity to spend time with a potential peer, it is cause for concern if he only asks a few questions.

Some candidates also show their true colors during this exercise. I once had a candidate ask a reverse interviewer, "Can I disappear on Fridays and play golf?" True story! No, that person did not get the job.

It is important that the interviewer refrain from asking questions during a reverse interview. Even though this person is not a member of the management team, the interviewer could create a legal risk for the company by asking an out-of-bounds question of the candidate. There isn't a necessity for this person to ask questions of the candidate as his questions are not the purpose of this interview.

Executives often ask how forthcoming the reverse interviewer should be with candidates when responding to their questions. The answer to that question is a question:

> Would you rather add a salesperson to the team who quits after three months because the job isn't right for him, or would you rather he withdraws from consideration before ever extending an offer because he determined that the role is not a good fit for him? Hint – One of these helps avoid a potential revenue investment disaster.

In addition to *Performance Factor Portfolio* matches, evaluate these aspects as well, just like with the other interviews:

- Punctuality
- Feeling
- Diction
- Dress
- Style
- Note-taking
- Next steps
- Questions asked

Mini-Business Plan

Chances are that the *Performance Factor Portfolio* includes a requirement that salespeople be adept at written communication. What sales role today does not require the salesperson to prepare proposals and exchange emails with prospects? While this is a highly critical skill, many salespeople are not strong writers, and most employers have no interest in teaching Writing 101.

It's not uncommon for me to hear frustrated executives expressing their embarrassment over the quality of the sales correspondence produced by their salespeople. Yet, none of them ever said that they evaluated candidates' writing skills before making revenue investment decisions.

To address this issue, let me introduce a candidate evaluation technique that is a personal favorite of mine – the mini-business plan. Once a candidate has nearly reached the end of the *RIEP*, request that he provide a mini-business plan in which he shares how he plans to make your investment in him fruitful. Leave the rest open to his creativity and interpretation.

When requesting the document, ask him to provide a *one-page* plan, just *one-page*, and only *one-page*. (Notice that I stated "*one-page*" three times as you should do when requesting the plan.) Finally, ask when he can submit the plan, but don't give a deadline.

Here's what is learned about a candidate through the use of this *RIEP* component:

1. How well the candidate understands the role.

2. If the candidate is philosophically aligned with the sales manager relative to his sales approach.

3. How well the candidate communicates in writing.

4. If the candidate listens effectively – as a one-page plan (three times) was requested.

5. If the candidate can meet a self-imposed deadline – as the candidate was asked for a submission date rather than given a due date.

In my experience, this component leads to more candidate fallout than any other component or hiring tool. It can be both an eye-opener and a deal-killer. One candidate misspelled our company name five times on a single page. Other candidates missed their self-imposed deadlines. Some submitted the second coming of *War and Peace* – despite my request for a single page. I've also had several candidates demonstrate an inability to communicate in writing.

Not all of these botched mini-business plans ended the *RIEP* for candidates, although repeatedly misspelling the name of our company certainly did. This component helps to understand the candidates' writing abilities when making revenue investment decisions.

Online Check

Since childhood we've been warned: "Things are often not what they appear to be," "Don't judge a book by its cover," and "Beauty is in the eye of the beholder." These expressions are reminders to look twice, to have a skeptical eye, and not to believe everything you hear or see. When it comes to candidates in the 21st century, these adages are probably more apropos than ever.

I had the opportunity to interview my good friend Sam Richter, best-selling author and founder of the *Know More!* business improvement program, about analyzing a candidate's online presence during the *RIEP*.

He provided valuable insights about the process, and I strongly urge employers to follow his advice. Sam suggests the following:

- Recognize that how people present themselves in interviews may not be the true or "real" person. Because the Internet has become a powerful, objective, verification check, employers should use it to support (or supplement) what the candidate shares. Before relying on the wealth of online information that you can gather, consider the following questions:

    1. Where is the information?

    2. How does one access it?

    3. Is it legal or ethical to do so?

    Nearly everyone today has an online presence ... whether they know it or not. If you can type someone's name into a computer and find him on a social network or in a general search, that information is most likely considered in the public domain and, depending on what is found, may even be used as a determining factor when an employer makes a revenue investment decision.

- Review a job candidate's online postings. This will show whether or not the person does the following:

    1. Communicates effectively.

    2. Consistently makes spelling and grammar mistakes.

    3. Is defensive and argumentative, or uses logic and facts to back up a point of view.

- Read the online information the candidate has written to describe himself. This information can include volunteer activities, charitable donations, professional associations, hobbies, and even details about his family. This information can be used to verify what is stated during an interview, and provides helpful insights into what a person is truly like as well his values and priorities.

- Visit the candidate's LinkedIn page. Many candidates will create a custom resume for a specific job opening. Yet, they don't update their LinkedIn profile. For example, a candidate's resume may claim that he played an integral role in the creation of a company's product. However, his LinkedIn profile may state that he worked at that company less than a year. The discrepancies are worth investigating.

- Consider reviews of Facebook and Twitter accounts to be fair game. A person's Facebook and/or Twitter postings will often show how he spends his free time and they may provide insights into his political beliefs, sense of humor, professionalism and judgment, as well as how he responds to criticism.

  For example, on Twitter and Facebook, many people will express strongly held views on a variety of topics from political events to social issues. These postings may or may not be relevant when determining if someone will be a good cultural fit within an organization.

- Do your homework before evaluating information found online. Before using Internet checks as part of your decision criteria, it is important to talk with both your Human Resources and Legal departments to determine what can and cannot be used.

In today's world, almost everyone has multiple personas – the one he shares in-person, the one he shares online, and the one others share online about him. The reason you may want to consider researching a candidate online is to determine if those personas are consistent. If they are not, at the very least, ask additional questions of the candidate. Depending on the law and what an Internet check reveals, an inconsistency may even be a reason to eliminate a candidate from the process.

You can learn more about this topic and Sam Richter at www.samrichter.com.

Professional Reference Check

An often neglected part of the *Revenue Investment Evaluation Program* is professional reference checking. It's easy to understand why. By sharing negative employment information about an individual, a company (and even the responding individual) can be caught in a legal quagmire. Thus, many references will say very little about a former employee and may stick to a corporate script. Hiring executives also recognize that candidates oftentimes provide the names of favorite co-workers, or others who adore them, as references.

While both of these concerns are valid, the reference component of the process cannot be ignored. The requisite due diligence is needed so that informed, revenue investment decisions can be made. For instance, much can be learned about the candidate based on the list of references provided. It is cause for concern if the candidate provides the names of peers and colleagues, but no former managers or corporate executives.

When requesting references, don't leave the question open to the candidate's interpretation. Share the specific type of references desired. Stating that you want "professional references" is too vague. Explain that you want to speak with his direct managers (or the manager's managers) and even clients (if possible). What is to be avoided are references that send you to Human Resources because they share little more than employment dates and titles. Plus, in most cases, the candidate has had little meaningful interaction with the HR department, so what valuable insight can they provide?

Going into the reference check exercise expecting an employer to bash a former employee is a total waste of time. Even if this person was horrible at sales, few references provide that much candor. You will have to creatively mine information from the references. There is one question I've found to be very effective – and it's a real door opener to the conversation:

> Given what you know about this person, in what type of sales environment would he thrive?

This question gets right to the heart of the exercise, which is to determine if this is the right person for this specific revenue investment. Typically, the reference openly shares information as there is no perceived threat implied by the question. The question isn't meant to be threatening either, but it does help further contrast the candidate with the *Performance Factor Portfolio*.

Reference due diligence has also evolved beyond the telephone. There are now ways for reference checking to be conducted electronically. Some firms have created a way for business references to provide online candidate feedback. These online reference providers have found that references are more candid when sharing information online which could be a helpful addition to the *RIEP*.

Having read through all of these component options, you may be wondering how long the *RIEP* should be or how many components are needed. There isn't a quick and easy answer to either of those questions. The *RIEP* should be long enough and have the requisite steps needed for confident, informed, revenue investment decisions to be made. If it's too short, it is highly likely that not all of the performance factors have been explored. At the other end of the spectrum, *RIEP*s that are too long create a risk of losing talented salespeople – a group not known for their patience.

Revenue Investment Evaluation Team

Imagine a strong salesperson is brought in for an interview and she asks the first interviewer, "What would you say is the company's biggest strength?"

The interviewer quickly responds, "Our customer service! No one is better than us when it comes to delivering service."

During an interview later that same day with another member of the evaluation team, she rephrases her question and asks, "What is one area of your business that you are trying to improve upon?"

This interviewer sheepishly responds by saying, "Well, our customer service is not where we want it to be, but we are working on it."

Ouch! This completely avoidable experience is not only embarrassing to the brand, but it also gives the appearance of company members being less than forthcoming with the candidate.

Companies often forget an important step when developing the *RIEP*, namely putting together a *Revenue Investment Evaluation Team* and preparing its members to evaluate candidates. For starters, all evaluators need a copy of the *Performance Factor Portfolio*. Without it, how can they effectively contribute to the decision-making process?

Evaluator preparation is such an important element when considering candidates for revenue investments. This preparation also helps the company put its best foot forward throughout the *RIEP*. Preparing the *Revenue Investment Evaluation Team* ensures that candidates are not scared off by inconsistent messages which give the appearance of the company not having its act together.

Below is a list of questions to talk through with the team to finalize the scope of the *RIEP*.

1. What are the components of our *RIEP* and in what order will the candidates participate in them?
2. Who is the lead person communicating with the candidates throughout the duration of the *RIEP*?
3. What is the expected duration of the *RIEP* from initial contact with the candidate to offer?
4. What is the timeframe in which the team wants to make a new revenue investment? (a.k.a. start date)
5. Who will ask which questions to expose synergies (or lack thereof) between the *Performance Factor Portfolio* and the candidates?
6. What information will be shared with the candidate, when, and by whom?
7. What are the expected questions that candidates will ask of the team and what will be our responses?

8. Who will respond to each of those questions?

9. How will the team gather feedback from the evaluators during and after the *RIEP*?

10. How will a revenue investment decision be made?

By going through this preparation exercise, the entire team will be on the same page when evaluating *Revenue Investment Candidates*.

Once a draft of the *RIEP* has been prepared and agreed-upon by the *Revenue Investment Evaluation Team,* review it with both the Human Resources and Legal departments to ensure compliance with company policy and law.

With your *RIEP* constructed, a step-by-step plan is now in place to evaluate candidates. The evaluation begins with the candidate's *Revenue Investment Prospectus* – a salesperson's resume. While the *Prospectus* offers insight into the candidate, it can also deceive potential investors. The next chapter teaches the six analytic points when reviewing a *Revenue Investment Prospectus* to separate fact from fiction.

8

ANALYZING A REVENUE INVESTMENT PROSPECTUS: A SALESPERSON'S RESUME

Over the years, I've seen more than five thousand salesperson resumes. I'm yet to see one that shows someone who has achieved 40 percent of quota. Every resume shows 100 percent, 200 percent and 2,000 percent of goal. The sellers have doubled, tripled and even quadrupled revenue based on what they have represented in their resumes. Where are all the salespeople who have had less-than-stellar sales performances? Did they all leave the sales profession? Maybe some found other jobs, but most are still in sales. If these sales resumes were an accurate representation of sales performance, our economy would always be booming.

When a company begins the process of considering a revenue investment in its sales team, the starting point is a review of a candidate's *Revenue Investment Prospectus* – a salesperson's resume. This "marketing tool" presents key information about the candidate so that executives can decide which ones warrant further consideration and participation in the *Revenue Investment Evaluation Program*. Oftentimes, the challenge is getting to the truth.

With traditional investments, there are legal actions and sanctions that can be imposed when a prospectus deceives potential investors. Those risks discourage misrepresentation of the investments. Unfortunately, that same protection does not exist when evaluating *Revenue Investment Candidates*. That means executives need to carefully scrutinize the candidate's *Revenue Investment Prospectus* using these six analytic points:

1. Generic. Looking at the resume's title, what type of position does it say the candidate seeks? A clear indicator of someone who merely wants a job is a resume title that says "looking for a sales or sales management role." These are two completely different jobs, which means this person just wants to be employed and doesn't care what job he gets. In Chapter 9, you will learn why this is a red flag.

2. Accomplishments. There is an old sales expression, "If you can't prove it, don't say it." This usually refers to the dialogue between a salesperson and a prospect, but it also applies to resumes. You are well within your rights to ask a candidate for documentation of the accomplishments presented in his *Prospectus*. If he doesn't have documentation, consider requesting a reference to support the accomplishment claim.

Checking every single accomplishment is over the top and unnecessary, but checking one or two is prudent. The ones that seem the most impressive about the candidate are the ones to be verified. If someone told me that he was personally responsible for doubling the size of the company in one year, I would want to see evidence of that feat.

3. Title. The sales profession has countless titles that describe the same roles and responsibilities. Remember, as you review each *Prospectus*, titles don't necessarily match with responsibilities. A small firm may refer to its only salesperson as "vice president of sales," while a large company may call a person performing the same functions "sales representative" or "business development specialist."

Don't get stuck on titles. Focus instead on the individual's responsibilities in prior positions, rather than the titles, to determine if there is a match to the *Performance Factor Portfolio*. If the resume doesn't clearly explain the role's responsibilities, those are areas worth exploring during the interview discussions.

4. Employer dates. If a salesperson has a gap (or gaps) in his career – meaning he did not leave one job and go directly to another one – he will often list years of employment, but not corresponding months on his resume. In other words, the *Prospectus* will show 2008 – 2013, not June 2008 – January 2013.

This creates the illusion of continuous employment. If a background check is performed as part of your *RIEP* and employment verification is part of that scope, this gap will be identified at that time. However, that takes time and dollars. Why wait until the end of the process to learn something that can be known now?

When years are presented on a *Prospectus* without corresponding months, ask the candidate to provide complete employment dates. Ask questions to understand the gaps. You may still elect to make a revenue investment in this salesperson given the explanation provided.

5. Training Programs. Many salespeople list training programs on their resumes, but who verifies completion and certification? No one does. When hiring IT professionals, it is commonplace to verify training and certification completion. This is not often done in the sales profession.

What risk does a salesperson take by stating on his *Prospectus* that he has completed the "Miller-Heiman Strategic Selling" course? There's no risk because no one asks for proof. Don't miss this verification step – ask for a copy of the completion certificate. If he has truly taken the course, you will see a confident reaction. If the candidate has only read the book, or perhaps not even that, he will start to squirm in his seat.

6. College Degree. When reviewing the education section of a *Prospectus*, expect to see college name, degree completed, and graduation date. However, sometimes degree or graduation date is omitted. Red flag! Again, a background check will expose that issue, but why wait to find out? When information is missing from the resume, ask the candidate if he graduated from the listed college, in what year, and with what degree/major?

A candidate may omit his graduation year to hide his age, but some do it to create the illusion of degree completion. Unfortunately, you will find some salespeople list a college and year, and hope they won't be asked any questions.

The review of the *Revenue Investment Prospectus* should not be taken lightly. By carefully reviewing each resume, only those candidates who are qualified to participate in the *RIEP* are invited. The *Prospectus* review is something that can be done by the Human Resources department – if the six analytic points presented in this chapter are shared with them. Hopefully, through these reviews, candidates have been identified for participation in the *RIEP*. The next chapter shows how to further evaluate these candidates with the goal of identifying those worthy of an investment.

9

EVALUATING REVENUE INVESTMENT CANDIDATES

Most executives say that evaluating sales talent is challenging – to say the least. For starters, they are attempting to evaluate professional interviewers. Salespeople know how to play the game, and the top ones are masters of it. They have the sales jargon down and know exactly what executives want to hear.

Further complicating matters is that the evaluation process begins with a flawed tool – the resume – as shared in Chapter 8. No two resumes are structured the same way or contain the same information. It is the *Revenue Investment Prospectus* that dupes, tricks, and stretches the truth of a person's background and accomplishments which is why the six analytic points are a critical point of the process. Unfortunately, this is the tool used to introduce the candidate to the company.

When it comes to evaluating candidates, some executives are optimists and look for every reason to make a revenue investment. Others are pessimists and search for reasons not to make a revenue investment. Neither of these philosophies is very helpful or effective when evaluating candidates.

There's no need to be an optimist or a pessimist given what has just been constructed. In earlier chapters, the *Performance Factor Portfolio* was created and the *RIEP* designed to identify those candidates with the potential to be great in a specific sales role. The process has now transitioned into a data-matching exercise. The *Portfolio* is on one side and the investment candidate is on the other. The exercise is a comparison of the two. There's no emotion involved or needed. Be pragmatic!

Your Job or A Job

As the *Revenue Investment Evaluation Team* members evaluate each candidate, a core assessment point should be in the forefront of their minds. They need to determine if the candidate wants any old job, or the specific job opportunity being offered. In other words there is a question that needs answering:

> Is this person seeking any sales job or is this person passionate about this specific role in the company?

I experienced an example of this when shopping at a novelty store in the mall. A job seeker walked into the store and requested a job application. The store manager told the candidate, "We don't have job applications, but go to any other store, get one of theirs, and bring it back to me."

When the candidate walked away, I asked the store manager why he didn't give out job applications, and he gave a fascinating response. He said: "There are so many people on the street looking for jobs that we use this technique as a filter to identify those who show initiative. After all, if he won't walk across the hall and ask for an application, how much effort will he really put into this position?" What a subtle, yet effective, way to identify genuinely-interested candidates.

Sales Rebound

In addition to figuring out which candidates want any sales job, another revenue investment pitfall to avoid is what I call *sales rebound*. Think of your dating days, whether in the present or past. While you may look back on those days fondly, you may also recall the moments when you decided that the people you were dating at various times were not right for you.

For teens what commonly happened next was dating rebound. They jumped from one relationship into another without fully evaluating their options. Rarely, was the rebound relationship a long-lasting one.

This issue isn't just child's play. When salespeople decide they want to jump ship from their current employers, they are often on the rebound. They aren't necessarily looking for the best options for their skills or carefully evaluating the fit of new roles. They want any options other than the ones they already have.

Just like the person on the receiving end of dating rebound, don't become a victim of *sales rebound*. The people who join your company for the wrong reasons won't stay very long either, which means the revenue investment will be flushed away.

Passionate Candidates

How do you know the candidate sitting in front of you is seriously interested in the role? Two reflective questions will guide you to the answer:

1. How prepared is the candidate for the interview?

The research they have done on both the company and you expose their interest in the role. Today, so much information is easily available online. Candidates have no excuse for being ill-prepared for an interview. Since a job interview is the ultimate sales call, a candidate's preparation indicates how he will prepare for sales calls if invited to join the team.

To quickly expose their level of preparation, I like to start interviews with this question: "What can you tell me about my company?" The shorter the answer, the shorter the interview. After all, if he isn't going to invest the time to prepare, why should I consider investing in him?

I'll never forget the candidate I met while consulting for a Minor League baseball team. We began the *RIEP* with a phone interview, but he clearly hadn't done his homework. I asked what he thought was a casual, passing question, "What was the score of last night's game?" He was stunned by the question and didn't know the answer. If he really wanted to sell for this team, wouldn't he have made sure to know the score before the interview? Practicing what I preach, I never call this client unless I am up to speed on the latest team happenings – which means taking just a few minutes to read its website.

2. What does the candidate want to know?

If the candidate doesn't have thoughtful – or any – questions for the interviewer, that's an indication you may want to look elsewhere for your next revenue investment. Given the level of importance associated with job searches, interested and well-prepared candidates will ask plenty of questions, including tough ones, so you and your evaluation team better be prepared.

Candidates passionate about securing a specific sales role in your company – that's a key to the success of the revenue investment.

Candidates Evaluating the Prospective Investor

I had the privilege of proposing to my wife in the White House. A dear high school friend, who was chief of a federal agency at the time, arranged for this surreal life event. On July 24, 1996, I bent down on one knee in the White House Rose Garden and asked Sharon to marry me. You already know her answer since I refer to her as my wife.

What if during the entire two years we were dating, I focused on getting to know her needs, wants, desires, likes, and dislikes – but never let her get to know me at all? What is the chance that she would have accepted my proposal? The odds are pretty high that I would not have been pleased with her answer. How could she be expected to make an informed decision if I had kept the relationship at arm's length?

This may seem silly to you. Who would propose without both sides getting to know one another? It happens every day when companies consider candidates for their sales teams. Executives are so focused on evaluating the investment candidates that they forget to turn the tables and give candidates the chance to evaluate them and the company. Having a reverse interview component as part of the *RIEP* helps to avoid this issue.

Here's a common candidate evaluation approach, but not one I would call a best practice. A company executive says: "We're going to bring the candidate in for an interview. If we like her, we'll bring her in for a second one. If we still like her, we'll make an offer."

Later the shocked executive asks, "What do you mean she didn't accept the job?"

When I led sales organizations, I didn't extend offers (take the ring out of my pocket), until both the candidate and I had enough information to make educated decisions. My expectation is that because we've gone through the *RIEP*, and I know the professional chemistry is there, I will get a yes.

The Candidate-Employer Disconnect

When executives look for *Revenue Investment Candidates*, they aren't searching for average players. They want the rock stars. Right or wrong, the search is for people already employed elsewhere.

What strategy do these executives use to attract candidates currently employed? They focus on enticing the candidate with an *opportunity* at their company. Then, these executives are stunned when candidates decline the job offers.

What they misunderstand is that while they are focused on the *opportunity* story, the candidate is grappling with the fear of *risk*. These candidates already have a job. While *opportunity* piques candidates' interest, the *risk* associated with giving up what they presently have can undermine the deal. "What if this new job doesn't work out?" That's the big question on the candidate's mind.

Think of the top salespeople you know. They hate change. Their compensation plan can be changed to raise the potential and, rather than be excited, they become uncomfortable. Positioning *opportunity* gets the candidate into the pipeline, but without resolving *risk*, there is no need to prepare the new office. The candidate is not coming your way. In other words this is just like any other sales process. When the sales strategy and buying strategy differ, no sale.

If implemented properly, the *RIEP* has identified a group of candidates who strongly match the core of the *Performance Factor Portfolio*. And, those candidates are excited about the *opportunity* presented and *risk* has been resolved. But how are revenue investment decisions made given all of the information gathered in the *RIEP*? Chapter 10 provides the decision-making roadmap.

10

MAKING THE REVENUE INVESTMENT DECISION

With several candidates having completed the entire *Revenue Investment Evaluation Program,* it's decision time. In which candidate(s) will a revenue investment be made? To answer that question, a determination of how the investment decision will be made is needed. The best place to begin the decision-making process is with a debriefing of the *Revenue Investment Evaluation Team.* Some organizations use candidate scorecards while others have open discussions to gather the team's analysis of the match between the candidate and the *Performance Factor Portfolio*. Both approaches work, so select the one that works best for your company.

When gathering feedback, some team members may make excuses for candidates who arrive late for an interview, have a less than polished appearance, or exhibit nervous habits during the evaluation process. Those issues cannot be ignored. What you experience with the candidate during the *RIEP* is their best. The dress will not improve, nor will the communications or written skills. If anything, these get worse once candidates become employees. So don't make excuses for the candidates. Base the decisions on what has been observed throughout the *RIEP*.

While each team member has shared his candidate analysis, the big, unanswered question is:

How will the revenue investment decision ultimately be made?

The answer to that question is complex given team dynamics and that committees are loosely formed groups often lacking a well-defined process for making decisions. If multiple management levels are involved, the process is further complicated as it is even more unclear who most influences the decision to invest.

Before the fate of a candidate can be determined, the team needs to set its decision-making process which is facilitated by answering the following questions:

1. Does one person's vote count more heavily than another's?

2. What if half of the team wants to proceed with the investment, but the others do not?

3. What if everyone thinks the candidate is a match, but the senior salesperson (who conducted the reverse interview) does not?

Again, there are many ways to resolve these issues. The key is to develop a decision-making process that aligns with your corporate culture.

Extending the Offer

After a comprehensive *RIEP* with a candidate, the finish line has been reached. The team is in agreement that the right candidate has been chosen for a revenue investment. The Human Resources Department crafts the offer letter, which is sent to the candidate for acceptance. A day goes by, and then a second one goes by, without a response.

On the third day, he calls with concerns about the offer. He's uncomfortable with the base salary and, while the letter says that the compensation plan is designed for him to earn a six-figure income at plan, it's still nebulous as to how that happens. Bottom line is that he is concerned which re-introduces *risk* back into the equation. After everything going so well during the *RIEP*, this candidate is about to be lost because a step of the process was missed.

If you've seen *Law & Order* (or courtroom dramas like it), you know that during closing arguments no new information can be presented to the jury. Extending an investment offer to a candidate is much like a closing argument. No new information should be presented to the candidate. The letter is merely documenting the elements of the offer already discussed.

One of the most common elements missing from a company's *RIEP* is the compensation and benefits review. Had that review taken place, the offer issue with the candidate would not have occurred. Quite frankly, *risk* cannot be fully resolved without sharing this information. Here is the way that compensation and benefits reviews are commonly handled:

When positions are advertised, candidates see: "You'll make six figures at plan. We have a full benefits program."

During the interviews, candidates are told: "You'll make six figures at plan. We have a full benefits program."

In the offer letter, candidates read: "You'll make six figures at plan. We have a full benefits program."

This may be a common method, but not a best practice when the goal is to have a high candidate acceptance rate of the offers. For the candidate to make an educated decision about the role, the compensation and benefits package needs to be shared *before* the offer stage. Since money is what a salesperson holds near and dear, not fully reviewing all of the role's financials causes trust issues and jeopardizes the potential relationship.

This financial review should, at a minimum, include:

1. The salary range
2. Compensation plan mechanics
3. Health insurance information
4. Benefits program overview
5. Any other factor that would affect the candidate's decision

The company should provide detailed examples that show expected sales results in the first few years in the role and corresponding income levels. For example, if the salesperson closes $250,000 in new business during the first year, he will receive "X" in commissions. By going through this exercise, the plan is brought to life for the candidate which helps him understand the different levels of compensation he could earn. Think back to the *opportunity* versus *risk* section in the prior chapter. By helping the candidate understand the compensation system, he is better able to put the *risk* concern to bed and focus on *opportunity*.

That said, be careful when discussing the earnings potential of the role. Money is a very delicate, dangerous subject. Why? Candidates may hotly pursue a sales role because they get super excited about the income potential. As a result, they may pay little attention to the key question of whether they have what it takes to be successful in the role to earn the projected level of income. While executives certainly want candidates who are money motivated, those who have the drive, but not the ability to succeed, need to be weeded out.

On the other side, I've encountered many executives who pursue candidates when they have not yet determined the compensation level or plan for the role. Believe it or not, this occurs much more often than one would think. Of course, this is not considered a best practice either. Before evaluating candidates, the compensation strategy needs to be determined, right down to the commission percentage that can be earned. Executives who cannot articulate the compensation package will unnecessarily lose candidates because the *risk* outweighs the *opportunity.*

While all of these steps may seem like small details, they are big decision factors for the candidates. When the compensation review is not part of the *RIEP*, two problems can occur. The first is a high decline rate because the candidate is turned off by the new information in the offer letter. This begs the question:

> Why lose at this point – after so much time and so many resources have been invested in this individual?

Similarly, when salespeople chase prospects for ages only to lose the deal because they can't meet the deal requirements, aren't executives furious? The same principle applies with these prospects, too. It is always best to lose early if you are going to lose.

Negotiating the Offer

The second problem that arises when the compensation and benefits review is not part of the *RIEP* is that the candidate wants to negotiate the offer. Since the dollars were kept hidden from him in the process, he thinks the offer is entirely customized and open for discussion. Then, a decision needs to be made whether or not to negotiate the offer. This is a tough situation. While you really want this person on your team, be cognizant of the relationship ramifications that could result if the offer is allowed to be negotiated.

If the decision is made to negotiate, think about the message conveyed to the candidate. He has just been conditioned to think that whenever the company puts something on the table, he should be prepared to push back and negotiate. For example, let's say he requests pricing to give to an account. He may be inclined to push back to get lower pricing given his initial experience with the company. Also, since this is a new relationship, this establishes a foundation that can cause mistrust. He will think the company is always trying to lowball him with the initial offer. Imagine how his annual performance review meetings will go and how he will respond to his performance bonus. Better be prepared for a painful, annual negotiation.

Remember, the ultimate goal is to create long-lasting, mutually beneficial relationships between the company and its salespeople. These are the investments yielding the highest returns. When it comes to offer negotiation, there isn't a standard right or wrong answer, but consider the ramifications before determining how to proceed.

Background Check

I was an executive in the employment screening industry for about a decade, so background screening is a hot-button issue for me. During my time with one screening company, we had an especially memorable experience with a candidate. This gentleman impressed everyone he met including the CEO. He completed our *RIEP* with flying colors. However, when we ran his background check (our core business), we found that his claim to have worked for a company for two and a half years was bogus. It was actually two and a half months.

Then, the fun began when we asked him about the discrepancy. He lied yet again and said that his former employer had made a mistake. Fifteen minutes later, he called back (I think he remembered that background screening was our core business) and fessed up. Needless to say, we couldn't have this person selling our employment screening services.

This is just one story. We saw several candidates flunk our background checks over the years. Consider this: If someone played these games when pursuing a sales job with an employment background screening company, what type of candidates are applying to your company?

In most cases, a background check is performed once the offer is made. Many companies use the background check to ensure a candidate does not have a criminal past, as well as to verify employment dates and academic degree(s). It is important to note that the background screening of salespeople should be different than the screening for other employees. This is due to the access salespeople have to sensitive company information, and the fact that the team members work independently and are regularly away from the office visiting clients. Consult with your background screening provider for counsel on the right scope for this role.

To learn more about background screening for sales candidates, download my free eBook titled "Are There Criminals on Your Sales Team?" at: www.SalesArchitects.net/backgroundscreeningbestpractices

Candidate Exit Program

Proceeding through the *RIEP*, the hope is that candidates strongly matching the *Performance Factor Portfolio* have been identified and offers extended. Unfortunately, that's not often the case. Most candidates will fail out of the process whether during the initial *Prospectus* review or another phase of the *RIEP*. Handling these candidates also requires care and planning.

How often does this happen in your company? During an interview, a member of your team says, "Nicole, you are a great candidate. We'll be back in touch with you shortly on the next steps." Days become weeks and Nicole never hears another word from the company.

While she is disappointed that she didn't get the sales job, she is even more irked by the way the company treated her. Guess how many people heard her interview story? When you've had a bad customer service experience, whether at the hair salon or in a restaurant, how many people did you tell? *Revenue Investment Candidates* see the interviewing experience as a customer service experience. As a result, they form opinions about the company and its products based on how they were treated.

If it takes a review of one hundred people to fill five seats on a sales team, five people are ecstatic. What about the ninety-five to whom offers were not extended? The most common answer is: "Who cares?" After all, they aren't the company's problem. Or are they? While the company passed over them for this role, care is needed relative to the candidate experience. A negative interviewing experience doesn't end with the selection decision. It becomes part of the pervasive perception of the corporate brand. Retailers don't make a revenue investment in every Tom, Dick or Harry, but they still want them to buy from their stores.

In addition, these ninety-five candidates are going to work somewhere. Maybe a competitor hires them. Or, one of the strategic partners adds them to the team. Perhaps, the company's largest client extends an offer. Does the executive team want these candidates spitting venom about the company in the marketplace? Of course not, and it's easily avoidable through the development of a *Candidate Exit Program*.

What's the biggest mistake companies make with candidates they decide not to hire? They go dark on them. In other words, all communication comes to an abrupt halt, leaving candidates to wonder about their status.

As part of a *Candidate Exit Program*, close the communication loop by sending a thank you letter. Advise the candidate of the decision to move forward with others, and wish him well in his job search. When a team member commits to following up with a candidate, make sure someone does. It takes an eternity to build a brand and a few seconds to destroy it. Don't let *Revenue Investment Candidates* exiting the *RIEP* damage the corporate brand. Take the time to develop a *Candidate Exit Program* and ensure the entire team follows it.

By this point of the book, you have learned how to make wise investment decisions for your sales team. But how do you protect the investments and get a fast, high rate of return from the new salespeople? That's a question answered in the next several chapters.

11

PROTECTING THE NEW REVENUE INVESTMENT

Eric, Vice President of Sales, spent the last several weeks evaluating candidates for an account executive position. At the end of the *RIEP*, it was obvious to the team that Ben was the right person in whom to make a revenue investment. When Ben accepted the offer, Eric was ecstatic about this new addition to the team. Anyone within earshot heard Eric touting Ben's amazing sales skills and looked forward to the success of his new revenue investment. Ben was going to be a game-changer for the company.

Three months later, Eric sang a totally different tune to his colleagues. "Oh man, Ben is gone. He couldn't sell anything." This expected sales star was fired because he sold very few accounts in his first ninety days with the company.

Apparently, there is an affliction that causes a new salesperson to suddenly morph from a superstar into bumbling fool. The disease has a ninety-day incubation period before becoming fatal to the salesperson's employment. The main cause for the affliction originates with the *great salesperson* perception embedded within the minds of many executives. It is this flawed belief that you can hire *great salespeople*, put your feet up on the desk, and watch the revenue roll in. If I had a nickel for every time I heard a story like Eric's, I would be a *gazillionaire*.

Assuming that the revenue investment decision was based on the match between the *Performance Factor Portfolio* and the candidate, the process yielded a salesperson with the potential to be great in the role. There is only one way for the salesperson to achieve his true potential for the company – and that is through *sales onboarding.* When a salesperson is added to the sales team, the hard work isn't over, it's just beginning for both you and the new salesperson.

Throughout this book, I've discussed the concept of adding a salesperson to the team as an investment in revenue made by the company. The *RIEP* is the approach used to select the right salespeople for the investment dollars. Onboarding serves as both investment protection and a means to get a high return on it. Salespeople joining the team arrive with a particular set of knowledge and skills. The essential onboarding experience is one designed to quickly help the new sellers leverage those skills in your sales environment, empowering them to perform at optimal levels.

Before going any further, let's define the term *onboarding*. Many see onboarding through the narrow lens of new hire paperwork and orientation. In essence, they define it based on the limited scope of the first day experience. Certainly that experience is key, but it is not enough. To ensure success, companies need onboarding programs that are comprehensive, methodical and customized. The most effective onboarding programs include both a step-by-step development plan preparing a salesperson to sell successfully for the company and an assessment of participant knowledge and skills mastery.

Salesperson Onboarding: Luxury or Investment Requirement

In 2012, I led a team of experts in a study of sales onboarding. Four key takeaways resulted from this study:

1. New salespeople need anywhere from eight months to more than a year to perform at the same level as their tenured colleagues. Yet, most employers devote less than two months to onboarding their new sellers.

2. Fewer than twenty percent of executives surveyed reported being satisfied with the amount of time it takes for their newly hired salespeople to get up to speed.

3. Executives most satisfied with their onboarding process have seen their new salespeople get up to speed four months earlier than new hires at companies that reported being less satisfied with their sales onboarding processes.

4. Executives who report the greatest satisfaction – and greatest success – with their new salespeople, have sales onboarding programs that are longer, highly structured, and comprehensive. From this outcome, we can then conclude that a longer onboarding process yields better results.

You can download the entire Sales Onboarding Survey Report for free at: www.TheRevenueAccelerator.com/onboardingreport

Getting Executives Onboard with Onboarding

Ever been awake at 2 a.m. flipping channels? At that time of the morning, there are countless infomercials selling exercise equipment. What do you notice about the actors and actresses in those commercials? Do you ever see unattractive, overweight people in pain? Of course, you don't! You see fit people - the results from the exercise program.

Imagine if the health club sales process sounded like this: "Your first day in the gym you are going to feel uncomfortable. The next day you will be in pain. The third day is going to be even more painful than the first. And, you won't experience any change in your appearance for about six months. Which membership would you like to buy?"

No one would ever buy a membership at a health club that emphasizes the work and pain associated with the fitness initiative rather than the desired results. These salespeople keep their prospects focused on the outcomes from exercise. Similarly, when it comes to sales onboarding program development, focus on the results that sales onboarding can have for the company. Focusing on the volume of work needed to put the program together leads to the sales onboarding initiative never getting off the ground.

Here are nine expected results from a well-crafted sales onboarding program:

1. **Revenue investment protection.** Throughout this book, I've shared the revenue investment philosophy when adding headcount to a sales team. Onboarding not only protects the investment, but also helps to ensure a high rate of return on it.

2. **Reduced ramp-up time for new salespeople.** One of the biggest executive complaints about new salespeople is the amount of time it takes for them to produce meaningful revenue for the company. By having a structured onboarding experience, companies reduce new-hire ramp-up time. Plus, the dollars invested before receiving a return are also reduced.

3. **Increased revenue performance.** Executives also complain that their salespeople cannot sell the value of their products, or that they can't sell the full solution the company brings to bear. Onboarding is the chance to teach salespeople how to sell effectively for the company.

4. **Improved client experience.** We've all been on the other side of the desk dealing with an inept salesperson. Because of our frustration, we were open to discussions with the competition. Onboarding ensures that salespeople are both equipped with the knowledge clients expect and are able to deliver a fantastic experience.

5. **Brand protection.** When salespeople cannot speak knowledgably about the products, the industry, etc., it creates a negative

perception of the corporate brand. Onboarding protects the brand by teaching salespeople what the marketplace expects them to know.

6. **Turnover reduction.** In the first year of employment, the most common reason for turnover on a sales team is that expectations are not met. Either the salesperson is unhappy with his income or the company is displeased with performance – bottom line is that this revenue investment failed and it's most certainly a financial loss for the company. Onboarding helps to minimize these instances impacting both the top and bottom lines of the company.

7. **Increased candidate pool.** How does onboarding increase the candidate pool? Many companies limit their hiring scope to just those salespeople with industry experience. The problem with this approach is that it further limits an already small pool of candidates. Chapter 3 presented all of the issues surrounding the candidate scope limitation of just those with industry background. Onboarding empowers you to consider strong sellers from other industries as well.

8. **Recruitment tool.** During the *RIEP*, there is often a concern of regarding how the candidate will get up to speed selling for the company. What is often not realized is that the candidate is wondering the same thing (part of the *risk* concern). Onboarding becomes a selling point that can help attract top talent and resolve the *risk* concern. It demonstrates corporate commitment to the candidate's success.

9. **Mis-hires found.** Sometimes, executives can be deceived during the *RIEP*. As shared earlier, salespeople know how to sell themselves. Onboarding provides the opportunity to identify concerns early in their tenure with the company and take action. This is true investment protection.

When is there ROI?

Those nine results clearly translate into dollars and cents, and a return on a company's revenue investment. The question is:

When will a return be received?

There are five investment milestones to monitor as part of sales onboarding. The timelines to reach those milestones vary by role and by company. The milestones to track are:

1. Monthly revenue produced matches monthly salesperson salary paid
2. Monthly revenue produced matches monthly salesperson cost incurred
3. Total revenue produced matches total salary paid to the salesperson
4. Total revenue produced matches total salesperson cost incurred
5. Monthly profit on sales generated matches monthly salesperson cost incurred

Consider the following example: A salesperson is added to a sales team at a base salary of $40,000 ($3,333 per month). The cost to the company, however, is not limited to his salary. Taking into account overhead, benefits, a percentage of his sales manager's cost, etc., this new salesperson represents a $60,000 ($5,000 per month) revenue investment to the company. Many executives don't consider the total cost picture, but they should to better understand when they will achieve, and then surpass, the breakeven point.

- If it takes five months for the salesperson to generate enough revenue in a single month to cover his monthly salary of $3,333, the company will have invested $16,665 to achieve this milestone (Five months x $3,333 salary).

- If it takes ten months for the salesperson to generate enough revenue in a single month to cover his monthly cost of $5,000, the company will have invested $50,000 to achieve this milestone (Ten months x $5,000 cost).

These first two milestones only represent a month-by-month look at the numbers. They do not represent the cumulative effect of the compounded costs, which are much more financially painful to the company.

- If it takes eighteen months until the salesperson's total revenue matches the total salary paid, the company will have invested $59,994 to achieve this milestone (Eighteen months x $3,333 salary).

- If it takes twenty-four months until the salesperson's total revenue matches the total cost incurred, the company will have invested $120,000 to achieve this milestone (Twenty-four months x $5,000 cost).

- If the net profit on the products sold by the salesperson is 20 percent, the seller needs to generate $25,000 in revenue in a single month to break-even on his $5,000 per month cost.

It is important to note that the aforementioned model is based on an annual salary of $40,000, and it took two years to recoup the full investment from that one salesperson. Obviously, these figures are compounded as each revenue investment is made. Also, companies pay salaries well beyond the amount in this model, which means a particular salesperson may not be profitable to the business for three years, four years, or longer. In addition, this example used a 20 percent profit on the products sold in the model. If the profit was lower, more sales would be needed by the salesperson to break-even.

Try the calculation using your own numbers in the free *Salesperson Profitability Calculator* at www.SalesPersonProfitabilityCalculator.com.

Given the business case and financial justification for a comprehensive onboarding experience, you might think that every company would have one. Unfortunately, that's not the case at all. There are two reasons why salesperson onboarding is not prevalent in all companies.

First, some companies haven't launched an onboarding initiative because they are not aware of the financial justification or business case. Without onboarding, these companies continue to "churn and burn" salespeople, even as they incur unnecessary costs and wait for the kind of sales levels they will never achieve.

The other reason why companies have not implemented a sales onboarding program is a lack of knowledge to create it. Hopefully, this chapter demonstrated why development of a sales onboarding initiative should be a no-brainer for your company. If your company hasn't launched one because the team doesn't know how, that excuse is about to vanish.

In the next few chapters, you will learn the steps necessary to create a sales onboarding program to both protect the investment and receive a high return on it. The onboarding development initiative begins with designing the salesperson's first day experience which is covered in the next chapter.

12

LAYING THE FOUNDATION FOR THE NEW REVENUE INVESTMENT

It's 8:28 a.m. when Brett arrives at ABC Industries ready for his first day as a salesperson for the company. He's excited, but also a bit apprehensive. Brett walks into the office, puts on a big smile, and says to the receptionist, "Hi, I'm Brett Wilson, your new salesperson." Looking puzzled, the receptionist responds, "New salesperson? I didn't know we hired a new salesperson. . . ."

Brett brushes off her response because it is not uncommon for the receptionist to be out of the loop when a new employee joins a company. She calls several managers, but no one knows what to do with Brett. He sits in the lobby as person after person walks by without saying a word to him.

At 9:10 a.m., Jack, Brett's new sales manager, walks in carrying a cup of Starbucks coffee. Jack greets Brett in the lobby and takes him to his new cubicle. "I'll stop by later and check on you," Jack says as he hurries off.

As Brett begins getting settled in his cubicle, he wonders if he is in the wrong place. The cubicle looks as if it belongs to someone else. He opens a desk drawer and finds a moldy sandwich. He opens another drawer and finds the performance improvement plan for the prior cubicle dweller. There's no laptop on the desk and the phone has the name "Phil" on the screen. All the while, employee after employee walks by, each taking a quick glance before continuing along. Brett hears whispers in the hallway. "Who is that guy in Phil's cubicle?" Yet, no one dares to step in and greet him.

Brett would love to get a cup of coffee, but has no idea where to get it. He also needs to use the bathroom, but doesn't know where it's located. He needs office supplies, but has no clue where they are stored.

The rest of Brett's day continues much like this. During his drive home, his wife calls asking how his first day went. Needless to say, Brett was not impressed by the experience. "Tomorrow will be better, I hope," he says.

First thing the next day, Brett is met by Jack. He had not seen Jack since being shown to his cubicle the day before. "We're so excited that you are here. You are the key to us blowing out our revenue target for the year," Jack says as he hands Brett a pile of papers. "Read through this information and you will be ready to sell tomorrow." Brett spends the rest of the day reading through the documents and taking copious notes.

On the third day, Jack greets Brett with a stack of leads and says, "You're ready! Here are a bunch of prospects. Now go sell!" While Brett has read every word of the "training course" he had been given, he doesn't feel prepared to sell ABC's product line. Nevertheless, he gives it a shot.

Brett's first month with the company does not go very well. On the last day of the month, Jack calls him into his office to discuss the results. "Tough month, I'm sure you will do better next month," Jack says. "Just try harder and you will be fine. Make more calls and the revenue will come." Brett leaves the meeting determined to show the company that he is the rock star they thought they had hired.

Following the pep talk, Brett spends the next month back on the phones – still chasing deals with very little success. Jack invites Brett in for another discussion about performance. "I'm getting concerned, Brett. When we hired you, we thought you were going to be awesome, but it's not happening. We need to see significant improvement over the next thirty days or ..." Jack doesn't finish the sentence, but Brett knows what he meant. Brett shares Jack's disappointment. He also thought he would be rolling in dough by now.

During Brett's third month, he sells a few new accounts, but not enough to save his job. In what feels like a whirlwind tour, Brett has gone from company rock star to unemployed dud. The blazing fire in Brett's belly that felt like an inferno when he first joined the company has been doused. He was ready to quit any way.

Whose fault was that disaster? If executives were asked that question, most would blame Brett because he was supposed to be a *great salesperson*. The underlying assumption – that Brett would somehow onboard himself into the role – is flawed. Let's further examine Brett's all-too-common story.

It seemed as if Brett's arrival was a complete surprise to almost everyone at ABC Industries. Yet, the sales manager was the one who extended the offer to Brett and set his start date. How could the company not be prepared for Brett's arrival? Unfortunately, most companies are not prepared for the arrival of their new salespeople. This lack of preparation has the potential to damage the relationship from the get-go.

Everyone remembers the first day on the job – whether it was a first job out of college or a job change. Most people probably don't remember their second day. But they forever remember their first one. That very first day sets the tone for the relationship. Think back, I'll bet you remember your first day with the company – whether it was last year or twenty years ago.

I've certainly had my share of first day nightmares. Several years ago, I was hired to lead the sales team for a technology firm. When I arrived on Monday morning, I was greeted by the general manager at the door. He took me to my office and said, "Well, I'll just let you go to it," and then walked off.

What I didn't know at that moment was that, up until Friday, someone else had been in the role – in that very office! This incident occurred before everyone had corporate email so no one in the company knew about the leadership change. People kept walking by my office wondering who I was and what happened to the last guy, including my now direct reports.

In another instance, I was hired to build out a division of a company. Upon arrival, I was puzzled by the response from the employees. Rather than being welcomed, it felt as if I had a target on my back as there was a continuum of people taking shots at me. How could I have enemies when I just walked in the door?

Nobody had told me during the interview process that, by creating this position, the company was transferring responsibilities away from several department heads to me. My role was a shock to the employees, and they did not understand why I was there as the CEO never explained it to them. They felt things were fine as they were. Several department heads viewed me as a threat to their careers.

Luckily, in each of these instances, I was able to persevere and succeed despite the poor onboarding surrounding my arrival. Fortunately, I was in management, which gave me the flexibility to navigate rough waters. New salespeople can't be expected to thrive in hostile territory.

I've heard countless stories from salespeople who were hired and then immediately encountered resentment from other sales team members. In some cases, co-workers felt threatened by the new salesperson, or they became hostile when management shifted territories to accommodate the new seller. In many companies, salespeople don't welcome additions to the sales team. You may see a smile, but it is usually a facade.

If this new hire were a staff addition to IT, Finance, or Operations departments, the person would be welcomed with open arms as an important addition to the team. That's not the case with sales. Often when companies add salespeople to the team, others worry that their own income will take a hit. While in most cases that perception does not match reality, it still needs to be addressed.

Getting the First Day Right

There's a common misconception that when a candidate accepts a job offer, he is fully committed. That's not the case at all. He hopes he made the right decision, but is keeping his options open. Don't think for one second that he has pulled his resume off the job boards and told recruiters that he is out of play. A key to employee engagement, the first day experience establishes the investment foundation. Will the foundation be set in concrete or quicksand? The choice resides with the executive team.

As part of sales onboarding, develop a plan that ensures a positive first day experience for the new salespeople. Here are tactics to consider for the plan:

First Day Game Plan

- Notify the receptionist so that the new salesperson's arrival is expected.
- Make the new seller's office so pristine that it looks as if it's never been used.
- Have the computer and any other sales tools ready before the new salesperson arrives – and display the correct name on the phone.

- Make sure all new-hire paperwork is ready on day one, particularly the payroll forms that ensure the direct deposit to his bank is correct on payday.

- Assign someone to introduce the new salesperson to the team members and show him around the office (e.g., kitchen, office supplies, restroom, etc.).

- Design an organization chart with photos, titles, and brief explanations of each employee's role relative to the salespeople (e.g., Steven David is the Vice President of Marketing. Contact him when you need assistance with proposals.).

- Have a documented onboarding activity plan ready and printed for the new salesperson.

- Send a welcome email announcing the new salesperson's arrival to company employees.

As George Bradt and Mary Vonnegut write in their book, *Onboarding*, "Design your new employee's experience as you would a client experience. People don't always remember what others said or did. They always remember how they felt." That's great counsel when crafting a salesperson's first day experience.

Remember Phil? He was the salesperson who occupied the cubicle before Brett – the one who left the half-eaten sandwich in the drawer. When he left the company, his co-workers organized a festive, farewell luncheon for him. What did the company do to celebrate Brett's arrival? Nothing.

Companies often have celebrations for employees as they exit, but do nothing for the salesperson who has just arrived. Celebrate the new salespeople and rejoice about the potential in the relationship. This can be as simple as inviting employees for coffee and donuts to meet the new salesperson. A small investment in the new salesperson can pay huge dividends.

With the new salesperson's first day planned, the next chapter presents the process of creating the rest of the onboarding experience. While many begin onboarding program development by identifying the curriculum, you will learn in the next chapter that the best place to start is at the end – with expectations.

13

IDENTIFYING NEW REVENUE INVESTMENT EXPECTATIONS

In the previous chapter, you learned how to create a positive, memorable first day experience for the new salespeople. Now a development program is needed to help these salespeople put their skills to work for the company. Every minute the salespeople are on the bench, unprepared to sell for the company, they are a liability on the books, a mere cost. Bringing in revenue is the core reason to have the salespeople. If they aren't able to sell, why have this large payroll expense?

Two Common, Yet Flawed Onboarding Approaches

Effective onboarding programs are structured to minimize the amount of time new salespeople are unable to sell for the company. Unfortunately, there are two prevalent sales onboarding approaches that create unnecessary risk for the investment and extend the timeline to receive a return on it.

The first I refer to as *Phone Book Onboarding*. This approach works something like this: "Hey, you're a great salesperson. Here's the phone book. Now, go sell!"

The other approach, which I call *Fire Hose Onboarding,* is the polar opposite of *Phone Book Onboarding*. With *Fire Hose Onboarding*, the company drowns the new salespeople in curriculum for a week and then sends them off to sell.

While those onboarding approaches may sound humorous, and may be even familiar, there's nothing funny about the results they bring.

Both lead to issues with the new revenue investment, as neither of them prepares the salespeople to optimally perform for the company. These two approaches lead to high sales turnover, underperforming sellers, and a constant mantra of "I need a lower price to get the deal done ..." from salespeople who lack the required proficiency to sell the product line at the desired price point. In short, the revenue investment is in jeopardy.

Beginning at the End

Given the issues with these two onboarding approaches, many think the onboarding development starting point is curriculum creation. They approach the project by gathering department heads in a conference room and white boarding the list of items for program inclusion. While curriculum development is an important part of the process, it is not the starting point. Two questions highlight the problems associated with starting the onboarding development initiative by creating curriculum:

1. Because content can be added for an eternity, how will you know when the onboarding curriculum is completed?
2. How will you know that the onboarding curriculum adequately prepares the new salespeople to sell successfully for the company?

The goal, when creating a sales onboarding program, is to ensure the new salespeople can sell effectively at the conclusion of it. Given that goal, the best place to begin the onboarding development initiative is at the end – by identifying the desired outcomes.

Imagine that Jamie has successfully completed the sales onboarding program. Executives, department heads, and colleagues now have *expectations* of her. Why? She is described as having successfully completed the onboarding program. These people become frustrated when she doesn't know what they expect her to *KNOW*, can't do the things they expect her to *DO*, and can't use the things they expect her to *USE*. Because of the *expectations* disconnects, new salespeople are on the receiving end of non-stop criticism.

> "I can't believe she doesn't know how that product works."
>
> "How come she can't deliver the corporate presentation?"
>
> "Why can't she use our ordering system?

The complaints go on and on. All of these issues have one thing in common; they stem from sales onboarding curriculum deficiencies. To avoid these issues, start the onboarding program development initiative by identifying *Revenue Investment Expectations* – defining the expected outcomes of sales onboarding. In other words, start with the desired end result. Three words give context to these *Revenue Investment Expectations*.

KNOW – DO – USE

The question to be asked is:

> If a salesperson has successfully completed the onboarding program, what does the team expect her to *KNOW*, be able to *DO* and be able to *USE*?

KNOW

This refers to *information* such as product knowledge, the competitors, and the territory. Some of the common *KNOW* expectations include:

- Who's who in the company
- Key roles and responsibilities
- Company history
- Organizational structure
- Key clients and case studies
- Go-to-market strategy
- Product features and benefits
- Industry
- Competitors
- Market position
- Ideal client profile
- Sales strategy and process
- Request for proposal procedures
- Implementation process
- Client support process
- Client pricing mechanics
- Client visit procedures
- Billing policies and procedures
- Sales compensation and mechanics
- Health insurance and employee benefits
- Expense policies and procedures
- Travel policies and procedures
- Sales collateral material for prospects
- Operations policies and procedures
- Style guide for written communication
- Social media policies

DO

This refers to *actions* such as conducting a sales call, delivering the corporate presentation, and demonstrating the product. Some of the common *DO* expectations are:

- Set up email and signature
- Set up phone and voicemail
- Order business cards and supplies
- Deliver the company's elevator pitch
- Generate leads
- Schedule a prospect meeting
- Strategically analyze an account
- Conduct a needs analysis meeting
- Correlate prospect needs with a solution
- Modify the corporate presentation
- Deliver the corporate presentation
- Create a proposal
- Develop prospect pricing
- Conduct a client visit at corporate
- Implement a new client
- Execute the corporate sales process
- Handle prospect objections/concerns
- Prepare an expense report
- Schedule travel
- Prepare activity reports
- Forecast deals in the sales pipeline
- Upsell an existing client
- Reserve conference rooms
- Conduct a client business review

USE

This refers to *tools* and *systems* such as a CRM, order management system, and demonstration software. Some of the common *USE* expectations are:

- Phone system
- Email system
- Copier
- Fax machine
- Webinar technology
- CRM
- Pricing tools
- Ordering system
- Intranet site
- Screen-share technology

This set of expectations drives the curriculum development process, which is shared in the next chapter. Using this approach, the onboarding curriculum becomes laser focused, and designed to ensure each *Revenue Investment Expectation* is met by the program participants.

Who should identify the *Revenue Investment Expectations*? There is a tendency to assign this task to one person – sales leader, human resources leader, or others. While having a point person for this initiative is critical to its success, the process is much more effective when a team collaborates on expectations, just like the *Revenue Investment 360* process. Involve executives and department heads in the process of identifying outcomes so that the portfolio of expectations is comprehensive and group consensus is reached. A little foreshadowing, stakeholder involvement is also important because their help is needed for onboarding curriculum and assessment development.

Having AN Onboarding Program – Big Mistake

With the stakeholders on the same page regarding expectations, the next logical step is to create an onboarding program. *Oops!* I just made the same mistake that most companies do when developing sales onboarding. I erroneously referred to "onboarding" in the singular form "an onboarding program." Sales leaders often tell me, "Every salesperson we bring on goes through the same program." And, they are proud of this approach.

These sales leaders should be commended for recognizing that new salespeople need a development program connecting their skills with role proficiency. However, having a one-size-fits-all onboarding program fails to meet the needs of its participants.

When the company makes a revenue investment in a salesperson, that individual arrives with one of many backgrounds – with industry experience, without industry experience, as an internal transfer (employee moves from another department to the sales team), or as a recent graduate. While the onboarding program length and curriculum must vary to accommodate for each of these backgrounds, the portfolio of expectations post-onboarding do not. In essence, the onboarding finish line remains the same, but the roadmap leading the salespeople to it varies based on their starting point.

Some examples of onboarding curriculum variance include:

- The new salesperson with industry experience probably doesn't need the industry basics during onboarding, but needs development in the nuances and advantages of the company's product line.
- The new salesperson without industry experience needs onboarding to start with the industry basics and terminology, but probably has a strong sales skill foundation.
- The internal transfer to the sales team probably knows the intricacies of the company (history, who's who, etc.), but needs selling skill development as the core of their onboarding.
- The seller just out of school needs a comprehensive onboarding program that includes both industry knowledge and sales skills.

A question that may be on your mind is:

How long should I make a sales onboarding program?

I don't have a standard answer for that question, because there isn't one. Three questions address why there can't be a standard answer for onboarding program duration.

1. What are the backgrounds of the new salespeople? (the four described earlier)
2. What sales proficiency will these new salespeople have upon arrival at the company? (sales veteran versus sales novice)

3. What are the expectations of the salesperson at the conclusion of onboarding? (*KNOW – DO – USE*)

For some unknown reason, three months (or ninety days) is tossed out as an appropriate duration for a sales onboarding program. Given the variety of responses to the three questions above, there cannot possibly be a standard duration for it. The best counsel is to create onboarding programs that are long enough to ensure every one of the identified expectations will be met by the onboarding participants. The next chapter teaches how to best design and structure onboarding curriculum to ensure each of the *Revenue Investment Expectations* are met.

14

GETTING A FAST, HIGH RETURN ON THE REVENUE INVESTMENT

In Chapter 13, the *KNOW – DO – USE* methodology was introduced as a way to categorize onboarding expectations. The focus now turns to onboarding curriculum development; the educational road map leading to each of the identified expectations being met by the participants. With the overarching objective of receiving a fast, high return on the investment, answers to three key questions shape the onboarding curriculum development process.

1. WHAT do the salespeople need to master?

To answer this question, the list of onboarding expectations is revisited. For example, in the *DO* category, an expectation has been identified as "adeptly conducting a sales call with a chief financial officer." The question to be answered is:

> What *Development Initiatives* (*DI*) must be addressed within the onboarding curriculum for the expectation of "conducting a sales call with a CFO" to be met?

The *DI* list identifies the areas for which curriculum is needed for the desired outcomes to be achieved. In this CFO example, the *DI* list includes:

- Needs analysis methodology
- Unique selling proposition

- Product knowledge
- Common concerns CFOs raise
- Competitors

Each of those *Development Initiatives* must be addressed in the sales onboarding curriculum for the new salespeople to successfully conduct sales calls with CFOs. Certainly, the *DI* list could be more extensive, but this paints the picture of the concept. Once the *DI* list has been developed for each expectation, the second question to answer is:

2. HOW will mastery be acquired?

In the CFO sales call example, the *DI* list has five areas to be addressed. Yet, how mastery is acquired for each one has not been resolved. That's the purpose of the second question. Identifying "how" can be difficult in some cases. For instance, if a company has not defined processes for parts of the sales function, how will mastery be achieved by new salespeople?

For example, let's look at the first *DI* on the list: "needs analysis methodology." What if the company doesn't have a documented needs analysis methodology? It begs the question of what will be taught to the new salespeople.

This scenario is not as rare as one may think. It's actually very common to find areas of the business where processes are not documented. Quite frankly, expect to find undefined processes as sales onboarding is crafted. This may appear to be a problem, but rather it's an opportunity to improve the organization. It does mean, however, that the process must be documented before the curriculum to teach it can be created.

Defining sales processes doesn't just represent a great opportunity to prepare new salespeople to sell effectively. It also helps elevate the performance of the existing sales team. Given that the overall sales team represents a major revenue investment for the company, one of the ways to get a fast, high return on it is through process development.

Two Curriculum Types

With the list of *DIs* identified and processes in place for each one, there are two types of instruction methods to assist with mastery: *self-directed* and *instructor-led*.

Self-directed refers to any curriculum that the salesperson completes without the involvement of others. The new salesperson is reading materials or conducting research on his own. Examples of *self-directed* curriculum include:

- Website review
- Competitor research
- Client case studies
- Tutorial videos
- White papers
- Industry journals
- Product specification sheets
- Organization charts
- Territory research
- User guides

Instructor-led refers to curriculum that is taught to the salesperson by others. In large companies, this might be delivered by a full-time trainer. More commonly, this instruction is delivered by department heads, sales managers, and sales peers.

When onboarding multiple salespeople simultaneously, a logical approach is to organize groups for *instructor-led* sessions. For instance, if the onboarding program includes training in the use of the company's Customer Relationship Management (CRM) system, it saves time and money to deliver the curriculum in a group setting. Moreover, group sessions reduce the burden on the staff and improve the learning experience for the participants. This doesn't override the necessity of unique curriculum aligned with the various salesperson backgrounds.

Another use of *instructor-led* curriculum is time with the sales manager. During onboarding, the salesperson and manager need to figure out how to best work together. Each salesperson and sales manager has his own unique style and idiosyncrasies. Onboarding is the time for the parties to build a productive, working relationship.

In addition, this one-on-one time should include opportunities for the sales manager to shine in the eyes of his sales protégé. For example, if the sales manager excels at delivering the corporate presentation, that's the person who should teach it to the new salespeople. It is a way for a sales manager to earn respect from his team.

Re-engaging department heads is also part of *instructor-led* onboarding. Early in the onboarding development process, colleagues were asked for their input on sales onboarding expectations. Now, their assistance is needed with creating and delivering onboarding curriculum. Who better to teach customer service than the head of customer service? Plus, this ensures there are no disconnects between the department head's expectations and the message communicated to the new salespeople.

Peer mentoring can also be an effective part of the *instructor-led* curriculum. However, it can be dangerous if not managed properly. The knee-jerk approach is to select the grizzled veteran to teach the new salesperson the ropes. However, that veteran and the sales manager may not be on the same page when it comes to effectively selling for the company. That person may have developed bad habits or may be selling in a manner inconsistent with what the company desires. Before a peer is asked to serve as a sales onboarding mentor, the sales manager needs to spend time with that individual to make sure they are in lockstep in terms of what is to be taught to the new salespeople.

The most valuable role the mentor plays is providing exposure into real-life selling for the new salespeople – which is why it is important to select the right person for that responsibility. Throughout onboarding, the mentor allows the new salesperson to listen to prospect calls and accompany him in sales meetings. During these sessions, the salesperson takes copious notes and writes down questions for follow up with the mentor afterwards. The sales manager should also conduct meetings with the onboarding participants to debrief on what was learned and observed.

The Delicate Balance

You may be wondering how much of the onboarding program should be *self-directed* and how much *instructor-led*. The most effective sales onboarding programs are a blend of the two types and that mix needs to be carefully monitored.

Onboarding programs with too much *self-directed* curriculum make the company feel cold and distant. Salespeople do not want to spend the majority of their onboarding isolated in a cubicle. As it is, the salespeople are chomping at the bit to sell even before they have been fully onboarded. Thus, if this is the approach taken, be forewarned that salespeople hate this kind of onboarding experience and get very little out of it.

On the other hand, onboarding programs that have too much *instructor-led* curriculum have issues as well. The people who are frustrated aren't the new salespeople. The irritated ones are those asked to train the new salespeople – such as department head colleagues.

A great example of this colleague frustration is the onboarding curriculum for the CRM. In many companies, there is one person who knows every intimate detail about the CRM and its functions. This is the individual tasked with teaching the system to the new salespeople. I refer to this all-knowing entity as "Yoda."

The salespeople arrive at Yoda's desk completely unfamiliar with the system. Yoda is not pleased as CRM training is not his full-time job. Since most CRMs have user guides, tip sheets, and tutorial videos, it raises the question:

> Why didn't the onboarding curriculum begin with a review of those tools (*self-directed*) before engaging Yoda (*instructor-led*)?

Had that been done, Yoda could have spent less, but more productive and focused, time with the new salespeople. Using this blended approach, Yoda's focus becomes teaching the system's nuances, reviewing best practices, and clarifying information that may have been unclear in the provided tools.

From a best practices perspective, *instructor-led* curriculum should be preceded by *self-directed* prerequisites. This reduces the amount of *instructor-led* time needed, improves the quality of the education, and makes mastery easier for the onboarding participants. This leads to the last of the three sales onboarding curriculum development questions:

3. WHEN is mastery required?

What salespeople need to master has been identified and methods for them to learn have been created. The temptation now is to cram the entire curriculum into their first week, and then send the new salespeople off to sell. That's a surefire way for the revenue investment to fail. It creates a high likelihood of never seeing a nickel of the investment back. Everyone wants revenue faster, but faster performance is not achieved by cramming the curriculum into a short timeframe. This is exactly what was meant by *Fire Hose Onboarding* in chapter 13.

This leads to answering the third question of the onboarding curriculum development process – *when* mastery is needed. Salespeople don't need to master everything on their first day or during their first week with the company. Even if you disagree with that statement, the truth of the matter is, the salespeople will not absorb all of the material in a few days. They will forget most of it as soon as the next topic is presented. For mastery to be acquired, information must be presented, reviewed, and reinforced.

The "when" is a very important point and one not often considered. When developing curriculum, the components should build upon one another. Balancing *self-directed* and *instructor-led* curriculum helps with that construction exercise.

Additional guidance in this design consideration can be found in Stephen Covey's book, *First Things First*. In this time management book, Covey presents a matrix contrasting urgency and importance as a task prioritization model. That same model is appropriate when developing onboarding programs. The entire curriculum is important, but which components are both urgent and important? The answer to that question serves as the guide for onboarding curriculum prioritization.

With prioritization set, the next step is to create an onboarding timeline and plot out the components. As the timeline is constructed, be sure to consider the amount of time it takes to complete each component. If this is not taken into account, there will be weeks with too little to do, and the salesperson will be sitting in the cubicle counting ceiling tiles. In other weeks, there will be so much to do that not even Superman could complete it all.

One final thought on onboarding curriculum development. Frequently, when executives evaluate revenue investment options, they look for individuals who are self-starters, and that quality is likely included in their *Performance Factor Portfolio.* Interviews provide hope that salespeople are self-starters, but that may not be the reality. Onboarding is a great way to determine if the new salespeople truly possess that trait.

To see if they are self-starters, don't constantly tap the new salespeople on the shoulder asking them to participate in steps of the onboarding program. Provide them with the expectations post-onboarding, the syllabus of curriculum components, and the due dates. Empower them to demonstrate their self-starter abilities.

This onboarding development process correlated expectations and curriculum with the primary goal of receiving a fast, high return on the revenue investment. To this point, we've only dealt with one direction of onboarding which is providing education to the new salespeople. The missing piece of the puzzle is the assessment of how well the salespeople acquired the knowledge and skills – and met expectations. In the next chapter, you will learn how to measure both participant mastery and curriculum effectiveness.

15

ASSESSING REVENUE INVESTMENT PERFORMANCE

Today, a new salesperson finishes the last component of the onboarding curriculum. What's next for the salesperson? In most companies, the answer is to send him into the field to start selling. While that is an option, it is not necessarily the best next step.

The onboarding curriculum provides education to the new salespeople – which is the most training and development that will ever be offered to them. Given that, the question on the minds of executives at the end of onboarding is:

Did the new salespeople acquire the mastery that was expected?

In other words, have they met the *KNOW – DO – USE* expectations as those are needed for a high return on the revenue investment to be received? The answer to that question is found by assessing onboarding performance.

The question of knowledge and skill mastery leads to the introduction of the *Revenue Investment Assessment Program* (*RIAP*). Both onboarding participant performance and curriculum effectiveness are analyzed using the *RIAP* through knowledge evaluations, sales call/group/CRM simulations, sales business plans, and feedback exercises. When you were considering revenue investments, the *RIEP* was used to contrast candidates with the *Performance Factor Portfolio*. Once the investment has been made, the *RIAP* is used to compare the new revenue investments' proficiency with *Revenue Investment Expectations*.

Knowledge Evaluations

While many wait until the end of onboarding to assess participant performance, information retention should be assessed throughout curriculum delivery. Administering quizzes after each major curriculum component is a great way to evaluate participant performance. At the conclusion of the onboarding curriculum, have a comprehensive, final exam to test knowledge of policies, processes, product knowledge, and the competition. In other words, this *RIAP* component shows if the *KNOW* expectations have been met by the onboarding participants. While having both quizzes and an exam may seem like extra work, both are important. Quizzes provide early warning detection of concerns with the investment while the exam is a final test of mastery.

Two types of questions are recommended for inclusion in both the quizzes and exam. The first is "fact-based questions" – those that assess information memorization. An example of a fact-based question is: "What year was the company founded?"

The other type is "application questions" which require the new salespeople to apply the information learned during onboarding in real-world scenarios. An example of an application question is: "A prospect has a concern about the price of our product, what steps will you take to resolve it?"

While it may seem easy to write quiz and exam questions, it is important to note there is a science to writing them. Before putting those questions to use with the new salespeople, ask the veteran salespeople to respond to them. Ask for honest feedback and use it to refine the questions.

Sales Call Simulations

Let's come back to the *DO* expectation example of "adeptly conducting a sales call with a CFO." How do you know that the curriculum fully prepared the new salesperson to handle that meeting? Maybe the salespeople didn't acquire the knowledge and skills needed to effectively conduct a CFO sales call. There is an easy way to find out if they are game ready. Rather than experiment with a real CFO prospect, have the new salespeople demonstrate mastery in your own offices during sales call simulations.

To put simulations into the *RIAP*, start by writing a realistic sales scenario. Since this is fictitious, the salesperson will need to be provided with all of the information that he would normally be able to find out on his own. With the scenario written, select someone to play the role of the prospect – the CFO. The CFO's character also needs to be scripted to make the simulation as realistic as possible. The character scripting should include:

- Setting his demeanor for the call – receptive or disengaged
- Identifying the challenges the "company" is experiencing
- Documenting the ideas and solutions to which he will be receptive
- Defining the end of the sales call for the CFO

To effectively evaluate the simulation, two or three evaluators are needed. During the simulation, the evaluators are seated behind the salesperson to avoid becoming a distraction. If the salesperson sees the evaluators taking notes, he'll be distracted and possibly lose focus on the exercise. Some record the simulation in lieu of having evaluators in the room – and some do both. A video of the simulation also helps the participant critique his own performance.

The unanswered question remains:

What should be evaluated and measured during the simulation?

While that answer may seem difficult to come by, it is actually already in your hands. It is the list of *KNOW – DO – USE* expectations. Review the list and identify the ones that can be measured in this simulation. Those expectations provide the information needed to create a score sheet. Many use a zero-to-five ranking based on simulation performance. From my experience, I've found that using a two-part scoring system in which one part measures *style* and the other measures *technique* helps effectively assess mastery.

In the Appendix, a sample score sheet is provided to help you develop a scoring system.

Group Presentation Simulations

For sales roles that include responsibility for delivering group presentations, it is recommended to have a group presentation simulation included in the *RIAP*. For example, if the team identified the *DO* expectation of "skillfully delivering the corporate presentation," it makes sense to see the salesperson's performance inside the company's walls – before letting him deliver it to actual prospects. It's the same argument as the sales call simulation.

Using the same example of the CFO, create a group presentation scenario that includes several people. Like the sales call simulation, each individual should have a scripted character. Select two or three evaluators for this simulation (and/or record it) and provide them with a score sheet based on the expectations list.

A sample score sheet for these simulations is also provided in the Appendix.

CRM Simulations

When executives purchase a CRM system, they do so having seen glorious sample reports presenting sales trends. The information in those reports is intended to empower the executives with the information needed to make business decisions. However, if the salespeople aren't using the CRM properly, receiving actionable data is nothing more than a fantasy.

If mastery of the CRM was identified as a *USE* expectation, a CRM simulation is suggested for inclusion in the *RIAP*. As part of the onboarding curriculum, training was provided (with the help of Yoda) on the proper use of the CRM. A CRM simulation assesses the salesperson's proficiency in the tool. It's easier to address training needs when salespeople are new rather than waiting for bad habits to surface.

In the Appendix, there is a sample score sheet for a CRM simulation.

Sales Business Plans

The new salesperson was immersed in the selling culture, methodology, and competition during onboarding curriculum delivery. He was taught company processes and best practices. He learned the attributes of the ideal clients and strategies to pursue them. Given that education, it is important for the executive team to know how the salesperson plans to apply that knowledge when in the selling territory.

Sales territory management has a major impact on the return on investment timeline. The wrong territory management approach can reduce, delay, or jeopardize the return on investment. Many companies leave this to chance and hope the salesperson manages the territory properly. Unfortunately, it is commonly found that the salesperson is not handling the territory as the executives expect. Once he's entrenched in his ways, it is very difficult to change his approach.

To avoid this issue, the sales business plan is recommended for the *RIAP*. The sales business plan is administered after the relevant on-boarding curriculum has been delivered to the new salesperson. This ensures that both the leadership team and salesperson are aligned with the approach to managing his assigned sales territory.

This sales business plan is different than what was presented in the *RIEP* section of the book. During the *RIAP*, rather than ask the new salesperson to create a sales business plan from scratch, provide a template. This ensures that the information needed to assess the territory management strategy is provided by the salesperson. Again, the information requested in the sales business plan ties back to *KNOW – DO – USE* expectations. Some questions to consider for the template include:

- What is your lead generation strategy?
- How will you determine which accounts to pursue and when?
- What do you feel are the attributes of the ideal client for each of our offerings?
- At what level in the prospect's organization will you begin calling?
- What will be your approach to scheduling a prospect meeting?
- How will you differentiate our offerings?
- Who are the largest competitors in your territory and what is your strategy to defeat them?
- Other than revenue, what metrics will you use to keep yourself on track?

Once the plan is submitted and reviewed, a meeting is held with the salesperson to discuss any aspects that may not be aligned with the company's vision for success in the role. That meeting helps to ensure everyone is on the same page as the salesperson is sent to the field to begin generating revenue.

Performance Management

For each part of the *Revenue Investment Assessment Program*, a pass/fail score needs to be set. That's the easy part. More challenging is determining the actions to be taken if a new salesperson fails to meet expectations.

One option is to end the revenue investment in the new salesperson before spending good money after bad. Perhaps, the team was fooled by great sales speak in the interviews. After all, the interview is the ultimate sales call. Although terminating the investment is not a desired outcome of the *RIAP*, it is sometimes necessary.

The other option, when expectations are not met, is to provide additional coaching and training. That's also why having a *RIAP* is so important. Without those assessment results, no one knows where the weaknesses reside. Without knowing the deficient areas, a coaching program can't be developed to address them and protect the investment.

It is also worth noting that if the onboarding curriculum is still in its infancy; don't be quick to fire the salespeople who fail to meet expectations. Provide coaching and development rather than letting them go. Early on, there may be disconnects between the curriculum and assessment. These will only be found as salespeople participate in onboarding. Once the curriculum and *RIAP* have matured, more aggressive action can be taken with the revenue investment.

Getting Your Onboarding Participants Focused

Let's play a little game. Put your left hand on your head. Jump up and down three times. Put your right hand on your nose. Spin around two times. Count to eight. How do you feel about your game performance? Do you feel like you are winning? Maybe you feel like you are losing. Actually, you have no clue how you are doing because I haven't shared the objectives of the game.

Oftentimes, executives don't share the sales onboarding program objectives with the new salespeople. The new salespeople don't know how they will be measured – other than through quota achievement once they are in the field. As a result, these salespeople go through the motions during onboarding rather than channeling their energy and focusing on the objectives of the game. Most salespeople are goal-oriented. Give them a goal and they will run through walls to achieve it.

To leverage their goal-oriented nature, present the sales onboarding program objectives to the new salespeople on their first day with the company. Share what you expect them to *KNOW* at the end of the onboarding program, what you expect them to be able to *DO* at the end of it, and what you expect them to be able to *USE* post-onboarding. In essence, present the *Revenue Investment Expectations* and let them know about the assessments that are administered along the way. When salespeople understand what is expected of them post-onboarding, they approach the curriculum with their eyes on the prize.

Rewarding for Onboarding Performance

To really grab the attention of the new salespeople during onboarding, offer a bonus payable based on *RIAP* performance. Their complete attention becomes focused on sales onboarding – developing a solid foundation to succeed for the company. Rather than paying a draw, which is either free money for the salespeople or debt to be repaid through commissions earned, invest in their mastery to motivate performance throughout the program.

Offering a bounty to drive onboarding performance isn't a theoretical approach, but rather a practice I've used several times when I managed sales teams – and it works! For example, I led a company's sales team in an industry that has a nine to twelve month sales cycle. Thus, the commissions earned in the first year of employment were thin. We implemented the revenue investment concept and developed a $7,000 quarterly bonus program payable based on *RIAP* performance. We scored the salespeople on their sales business plans, quizzes, exams, sales call simulations, and group simulations. The scores on each of the parts determined the amount of the bonus paid.

Some think this is a lot to pay a salesperson who has not generated any sales. However, our perspective was that if we could get these new salespeople focused on onboarding, they would ultimately sell more and faster – and stay with the company long-term. And they did! Consider how much it costs to hire a salesperson and the financial impact on the company if that salesperson were to fail. On the other side of the equation, think about the potential for the company if the new salesperson sells more, faster? For us, this onboarding performance bonus was a low risk proposition.

Feedback on the Investment

Not only does the individual salesperson represent an investment for the company, but the entire onboarding development initiative does as well. The team spent countless hours (which translates into significant dollars) putting this together. So, not only are the onboarding participants on trial after the curriculum has been completed, but so is the onboarding curriculum – especially when the program is still in its infancy.

To gain the most benefit from sales onboarding programs, they need to be regularly reassessed and tweaked so that they evolve with changes in the company, the product mix, and the marketplace. Otherwise, the curriculum becomes ineffective in helping to ensure expectations are achieved.

One of the ways to ensure the curriculum remains aligned with expectations is through a participant feedback program. Each salesperson has completed the program and can provide thoughts and recommendations to help improve it for future participants. Those involved in the *instructor-led* curriculum and direct managers of the new salespeople should also be asked to provide their perspectives.

The participant feedback program is to be administered twice. The first time is immediately after the salesperson completes onboarding. The second is after the salesperson has been in the field for an extended period of time. Ninety days after onboarding completion is a good measurement point for the second feedback session.

Why does feedback need to be solicited twice? If an onboarding participant, who has just finished the program, was asked how well the curriculum prepared him to sell, he would not know. He just completed onboarding and hasn't been selling yet. He will have meaningful insight to share after three months in the field.

What can be learned from participants who just finished the onboarding program is their level of confidence when performing the various sales functions. If confidence concerns are uncovered, that could indicate that some parts of the curriculum were too short or insufficient.

Certain questions should be asked of new salespeople who just completed onboarding and again after ninety days in the field. This is done twice because sometimes an onboarding participant's perception can change over time.

Participants can share feedback with the company in many ways including: one-on-one interviews, surveys, or a combination of the two. Any of these options can be effective depending on the positioning of the exercise. If the goal is to receive open and honest information, be sure the participants know they can provide feedback without any retribution. Here are some questions for consideration in the participant feedback program.

Immediately after onboarding program completion:

- Do you feel the mix between *self-directed* and *instructor-led* curriculum was appropriately balanced? If you answered no, what would you change?
- How much time did you spend each week with your sales manager?
- Do you feel you had enough one-on-one time with your sales manager?
- How did you feel about the pace of the program?
- How would you describe the level of support received from your Mentor? What, if anything, would you change?

Immediately after onboarding program completion and post 90-days:

- What curriculum would you add to the onboarding program?
- What curriculum would you eliminate from the onboarding program?
- Which onboarding components were too short or inadequate?
- Which onboarding components were too long?
- How would you describe your level of confidence when selling for the company?
- What recommendations do you have to improve the onboarding experience for our new salespeople?

Post 90-days:

- How well did the onboarding curriculum prepare you to sell for the company?

- How well did the onboarding curriculum prepare you for the quizzes, exam, and simulations?

Another way to ensure the program aligns with corporate objectives is to set onboarding metric goals and measure performance against them. Start by benchmarking the performance of the current sales team. With that baseline data, set onboarding performance goals for new, revenue investments. Some metrics for consideration in your revenue investment performance scorecard include:

- Start date to a salesperson's first sale date – reduced

- Number of sales in first year of employment – higher

- Prospect pipeline for second year of employment – higher

- Number of sales in second year of employment – higher

- Effectiveness in selling the full suite of products – higher

- Product sale price versus list price – higher

- Employment turnover within a seller's first year – reduced

Through feedback and metric management, the information needed to continually evolve the program and ensure it meets expectations is in your hands.

Parting Thoughts

Putting together a comprehensive onboarding experience for new salespeople can feel overwhelming. Some companies don't have the resources to launch an onboarding initiative as thorough as what has been presented in this book. That doesn't mean abandon the effort.

Instead, identify problematic areas of the business that could be remedied through sales onboarding. These should be areas that, if addressed, would produce a high rate of return on the revenue investment. For those, develop onboarding curriculum. For example, if "conducting needs analysis discussions" has been identified as a high impact area that new salespeople struggle to master, focus on fixing that through curriculum development. As time permits and with feedback, additions can be made to the program.

The methodology you have just read about will position the company, not just for growth, but for highly profitable growth. The revenue investment concept doesn't end when the salespeople are hired and have completed onboarding. It continues throughout their employment with the company. When you compensate them, every commission check should be written with the continued goal of receiving a high return on your revenue investment. When you manage the salespeople, manage them as if you are an investor in their businesses – because you are.

APPENDIX

GLOSSARY

1. **Revenue Investment** – a common business expression which this book uses as a reference to each member of a sales team. While adding headcount to a sales team is commonly viewed as "hiring," this book introduces the concept of investing in revenue.

2. **Salesperson Profitability Calculator** – the tool that exposes five investment milestones to be monitored with each new salesperson. Visit www.SalespersonProfitabilityCalculator.com to determine your company's revenue investment milestones.

3. **Revenue Investment Candidate (RIC)** – a sales candidate who is being considered for employment (*revenue investment*) with a company.

4. **Revenue Investment 360** – the process through which the performance factors for a specific sales role are identified.

5. **Performance Factor Portfolio (PFP)** – the set of factors that lead to sales success or failure; and are prioritized between *required* and *desired* attributes. *Revenue Investment Candidates* are compared and contrasted with the *Portfolio* in search of matches during the *Revenue Investment Evaluation Program*.

6. **Revenue Investment Evaluation Program (RIEP)** – the program used to identify the matches between the *Performance Factor Portfolio* and a *Revenue Investment Candidate*.

7. **Revenue Investment Evaluation Team (RIET)** – the people chosen to administer the *Revenue Investment Evaluation Program* leading to the determination of candidate investment decisions.

8. **Revenue Investment Prospectus** – this is traditionally referred to as a salesperson's resume. It is used to begin the evaluation process relative to the *Performance Factor Portfolio*.

9. **Candidate Exit Program** – the program used to protect the corporate brand when a decision is made not to offer a candidate a sales position with the company.

10. **Revenue Investment Expectations** – the identification of anticipated outcomes of a sales onboarding program using the *KNOW – DO – USE* methodology as a means to categorize each expectation.

11. **Development Initiatives (DI)** – are used to identify the onboarding curriculum needed for each of the *Revenue Investment Expectations* to be met.

12. **Revenue Investment Assessment Program (RIAP)** – the program used to measure both onboarding participant performance and curriculum effectiveness through knowledge evaluations, sales call/group/CRM simulations, sales business plans, and feedback exercises.

TOP 100 SALESPERSON INTERVIEW QUESTIONS

Below is a pool of interview questions for use with sales candidates. Should you ask all of them? No! Ask only the ones that expose synergies between the *Performance Factor Portfolio* and the candidates to help determine matches. The questions are not presented in any particular order.

1. Since you have decided to make a job change, what criteria are you using to select your next employer?

2. What can you tell me about our company?

3. From reviewing our website, what is one change you would suggest we make to the site and why?

4. Having learned about our company (pre-interview), what opportunities do you feel we are missing?

5. What steps did you take to prepare for this interview today?

6. Why do you feel you are the best person for this role?

7. Share an experience when you lost a sale. What did you learn from it?

8. What three words would your sales manager use to describe you?

9. How do you generate leads?

10. When prospecting, what is your approach to setting a meeting?

11. Why do you think people buy from you?

12. No one is perfect. What is one thing you are working to improve?

13. What do you do to improve your sales skills?

14. How do you research prospects before calling them?

15. What three words would your sales peers use to describe you?

16. If I were to speak with your manager, what would he say is your major weakness?

17. If I were to speak with your manager, what would he say is your biggest strength?

18. What was your greatest sales achievement? What made it special?

19. What do you feel it takes to be successful in sales?

20. What gets you out of bed and excited to start the day?

21. Why did you select "sales" as your career choice?

22. In your current sales role, how do you qualify an opportunity?

23. Share a goal that you set and how you achieved it. To what do you attribute your success?

24. Share a goal that you set, but failed to achieve. Why did you fail? What did you learn from the experience?

25. Share a time when your flexibility was challenged. How did you deal with that?

26. Part of what makes our company successful is being responsive to the marketplace, which means constant change. How do you deal with change?

27. How do you stay organized?

28. Describe your ideal sales culture.

29. Describe your ideal sales manager.

30. How will you get up to speed with our company?

31. What is it about your background and skills that tell you this opportunity is a great fit for you?

32. What do you feel causes a salesperson to fail?

33. What do you think it takes to be successful in this sales role?

34. What message do you leave on a prospect's voice mail to receive a return call?

35. Rejection is a big part of sales. How do you recover from it?

36. How do you defeat your top competitor also known as the status quo?

37. What is your income goal for this year? What did you earn last year? What is your goal for next year?

38. Where do you see your sales career in five years?

39. Share a time when you had to "fight" internally to get your sale completed? What obstacles did you have to overcome? How did you do it?

40. What's the most common objection you hear when selling for your current company? How do you handle it?

41. What is it about this opportunity that intrigues you?

42. If you won the lottery, what would you do?

43. What CRMs have you used in the past and how have they helped you sell more?

44. In your current and past sales roles, who were the ultimate decision-makers (level) for your offering?

45. How do you manage your territory to ensure you call on the right prospects at the right time?

46. Describe a time when you had a conflict with a peer. How did you resolve it?

47. In your current sales position, what metrics do you use to keep yourself on track to achieve the annual sales goal?

48. Share a time when you had to come up with a creative solution for a prospect.

49. How do you personally create value for your clients?

50. Why are you planning to leave your current sales role?

51. What do you like least about your current sales manager?

52. Describe your typical sales day (or week)?

53. How much time do you dedicate to prospecting for new business each week?

54. Describe a time when you had a frustrated, upset client who was on the brink of leaving for a competitor. How did you handle it? What was the outcome? What did you learn?

55. Share with me a time when you developed an account from scratch. Walk me step-by-step through the chronology of events that ultimately led to your company being awarded the account.

56. How would you describe your selling style?

57. How do you stay up to speed on the news and trends in your industry?

58. What sales websites do you visit to refine your craft?

59. What business book has had the most influence on your sales career?

60. What is the largest sale you have ever won?

61. Share a time when you took a small, current client account and turned it into a large one.

62. What three adjectives would you use to describe your ideal sales manager?

63. What one factor do you attribute to your success?

64. What is your sales call preparation plan?

65. Share a time when you had to use multiple internal resources to win an account.

66. What would be your plan to learn our industry?

67. Do you prefer to work alone or with teams? Why?

68. Who was your best mentor? How did he or she impact you?

69. Under what management style do you thrive?

70. Have you been successful building a referral-based business? What is your strategy?

71. What makes you unbeatable? (ask for examples)

72. Share a time when your competitor was in the lead, but you overcame the company and won the account.

73. What is your Sunday evening routine?

74. Share a time when you had to break the rules. What was the outcome?

75. Given the choice of being liked or winning, which would you prefer? Why?

76. How do you feel salespeople should be managed?

77. Share a time when your ethics were challenged. What was the outcome?

78. If we were to extend an offer to you, what would you want to know to make an educated, informed decision?

79. In your current sales role, what are your goals for the first meeting with a prospect?

80. Given the choice of a sales role or a sales manager role, which would you prefer? Why?

81. Since there are a number of influencers in the sale of our product, what is your process to navigate through an account?

82. Do you feel the Internet will make salespeople go the way of the dinosaur?

83. If you were selling for a company and making a lucrative income, but the product quality was poor, would you continue to sell for that company?

84. Describe a time when you took a leadership role (at work or outside of work). What did you accomplish? What did you learn from the experience?

85. Describe a time when you were outsold by the competition. How did it happen? What did you learn from the experience?

86. How do you define "success?"

87. What is your approach when working with procurement agents?

88. When you look at the sales profession, what changes do you foresee in the near future?

89. What changes have you made in your selling approach in the last few years?

90. What experience have you had in generating leads (and sales) from trade shows?

91. How have you used social media to generate leads?

92. We have two available sales roles in our company. One is primarily responsible for expanding the revenue relationship with our clients. The other role is a pure business development role starting from scratch. The first role pays more in the first two years,

but the other role has the potential to be much more lucrative in future years. Which role interests you most? Why?

93. Scenario: Upon submitting a proposal to a client, she balks at the price. What is your resolution approach?

94. Scenario: After building a relationship with a prospective client, it becomes apparent that this person does not have the power to make a buying decision. What do you do?

95. Scenario: Out of the blue, a request for proposal (RFP) appears on your desk. You and your company have no history with this company. What is your blind RFP strategy?

96. Scenario: Your proposal has been selected as a finalist and you are invited to make a group presentation. What is your approach to prepare for the finalist presentation?

97. Scenario: While working with a prospect, you recognize that he needs a particular product offered by your company, but your company also offers a higher-priced one that pays a higher commission to the salesperson. You could probably sell the more expensive product to the prospect. What do you do?

98. Scenario: During a prospecting session, you encounter someone who immediately wants to know the price. If you give the price, you will lose because you are a high-priced provider but offer significant advantages over the competition. If you don't give the price, the prospect hangs up the phone frustrated. What do you do?

99. Scenario: In your work with a prospect, you uncover that the company does not have a budget for your solution. What do you do?

100. What questions do you have for me?

Sample Sales Call Simulation Score Sheet

Style	0	1	2	3	4	5
1. Accurate						
2. Comprehensive						
3. Creative						
4. Engaging						
5. Clear						
6. Confident						
7. Articulate						
8. Passionate						
9. Personable						
10. Credible						

Score _____/50

Technique	0	1	2	3	4	5
1. Confirmed time allotted for meeting						
2. Proposed meeting agenda						
3. Identified challenges						
4. Probed interest in resolving challenges						
5. Positioned correct solutions for challenges						
6. Identified decision process						
7. Identified decision timeframe						
8. Identified decision influencers						
9. Handled concerns						
10. Defined next steps						

Score _____/50

Sample Group Presentation Simulation Score Sheet

Style	0	1	2	3	4	5
1. Accurate						
2. Comprehensive						
3. Creative						
4. Engaging						
5. Clear						
6. Confident						
7. Articulate						
8. Passionate						
9. Personable						
10. Credible						

Score _____/50

Technique	0	1	2	3	4	5
1. Confirmed time allotted for presentation						
2. Facilitated participant introduction						
3. Proposed agenda						
4. Identified participant meeting goals						
5. Incorporated goals into presentation						
6. Included sales call information into presentation						
7. Delivered presentation accurately						
8. Demonstrated active listening and engaged participants						
9. Handled concerns						
10. Defined next steps						

Score _____/50

Sample CRM Simulation Score Sheet

Technique	0	1	2	3	4	5
1. Create an account						
2. Create a contact						
3. Create a task						
4. Complete a task						
5. Insert a note in a record						
6. Forecast a deal						
7. Move a deal through the forecast process						
8. Complete a sale						
9. Run reports						
10. Search the database						

Score _____/50

Made in the USA
Lexington, KY
30 March 2017